See the Light

The Loving Light Books Series

Book 1: God Spoke through Me to Tell You to Speak to Him
Book 2 & 3: No One Will Listen to God & You are God
Book 4: The Sun and Beyond
Book 5: The Neverending Love of God
Book 6: The Survival of Love
Book 7: We All Go Together
Book 8: God's Imagination
Book 9: Forever God
Book 10: See the Light
Book 11: Your Life as God
Book 12: God Lives
Book 13: The Realization of Creation
Book 14: Illumination
Book 15: I Touched God
Book 16: I and God are One
Book 17: We All Walk Together
Book 18: Love Conquers All
Book 19: Come to the Light of Love
Book 20: The Grace is Ours

Also by Liane Rich

The Book of Love
For the Love of God: An Introduction to God
For the Love of Money: Creating Your Personal Reality
Your Individual Divinity: Existing in Parallel Realities
For the Love of Life on Earth
Your Return to the Light of Love: a guidebook to spiritual awakening

Loving Light

Book 10

See the Light

Liane Rich

The information contained in this book is not intended as a substitute for professional medical advice. Neither the publisher nor the author is engaged in rendering professional advice to the reader. The remedies and suggestions in this book should not be taken, or construed, as standard medical diagnosis, prescription or treatment. For any medical issue or illness consult a qualified physician.

Loving Light Books

ISBN 13: 978-1-878480-10-1
ISBN 10: 1-878480-10-3

Loving Light Books:
www.lovinglightbooks.com

Also Available at:
Amazon: www.amazon.com
Barnes & Noble: www.barnesandnoble.com

for Janie

The information in this series is not necessarily meant to be taken literally. It is meant to *shift* your consciousness....

Foreword

Anyone immersed in the vast body of new metaphysical knowledge is aware of the virtual symphony of voices from channeled sources throughout the world – inspirational voices that may be artistic, poetic, philosophical, religious, or scientific. And now, out of these myriad New Age voices, comes a series of books by God, channeled through Liane, revealing the frank truth in all its glory and wonder, telling us how to cleanse our bodies, gain access to our subconscious minds, clear our other selves and march back to who we are – God.

In God's books you will be introduced to a loving, powerful, gripping, exciting, and often humorous voice that reaches out and speaks ever so personally to the individual reader. As the reader's interest deepens, invariably an intimate relationship to this voice develops. It is a relationship that lasts forever, and I am quite certain I do mean forever.

Here is an accelerated program, a no-holds-barred course, where God guides us and loves us, and as needs be recommends books to us and even a movie or musical piece along the way. He (She) enters our lives and sees through our eyes, seeming to enjoy the ride as He guides us back to US, back to ALL. Here is a voice that is playful and informative, that is humorous and serious, that is gentle and powerfully divine. It is a voice that knows no barriers or restrictions, a straightforward and honest voice that caresses us when we need the warmth and pushes us when we are immobilized.

In today's New Age literature there is an avalanche of information from magnificent beings of light, information that possesses us and compels us to look at our fears and express our love. In this series of books by God, you will find truly powerful methods for making this transition from toxicity to purity, from density to light, from fear to love, and from the delusion of death to the awakening to full life. You will experience in these books the love and the power of God for it is your love to express and your power to behold. Rarely will you see more lucid steps for transformation. Read these beautiful words and rejoice in our period of awakening, our return to Home.

John Farrell, PhD., LCSW. – Psychologist, Clinical Social Worker, Senior Clinician Psychiatric Emergency Services, U.C. Davis Medical Center, Sacramento. John is also a retired Professor – California State University, Sacramento, in Health Sciences and Psychology.

See the Light

Preface

Once upon a time I did not believe it possible to be God. I thought only that it was me and it was not my permanent place. I was often surprised and even overwhelmed at all the possibilities. After all, it is not everyday that you discover your true identity.

You are often told that you are not who you believe and you are often told to love. You do not know how to love because you forgot that your true identity is love. *God is love.* God is nothing more than love and nothing is here except love. This gives you a very good option for discovery. You may only discover your own truth and your own identity, and since love is you and you are love, you have nothing to lose in giving up your false identity. You will lose your insecurities and you will lose your freedom to believe in how awful you are.

Once you have given up your identity and have chosen to let God (or love) shine through, you will begin to rise – rising like a morning star on the horizon of heaven. You will become God in God. Now of course you are God in matter only because you chose to be unconscious and not know your God-self. As soon as you begin to remember, you will begin to *feel* God (or love) growing within you once again.

The only reason you do not remember that you are love is that you have a block in your memory. Get the blocks out and voila`! You now have light, or God, or truth, or self-expression at its purest. You are not evil and evil does not exist. You are not bad and bad does not exist. You are not dark and darkness does not exist. Only good exists because only God exists. Nothing is outside of God. God is *all.* Space, time, light, illusion is all inside of God. Wake up! You simply fell asleep and began to create shadows that don't really exist. Stop blaming you for being unconscious. You went under for a reason and now you are coming out for a reason.

As you rise up you will begin to know that the illusion is but a fragment of what is. You are but a fragment of what is. When you rise you feel different in that you begin to feel indestructible. You begin to no longer concern yourself with pain, as you will know that pain is the illusion to keep you in place. You will see how knowing your own self is not so frightening and you will even find great relief from pain by letting your pain express and deplete itself.

Often you will find that in order to recognize your true identity you must fulfill some commitment you created in order to go under. You are simply knocked out and now you are coming to. You do not know who you are immediately and your memory may take time to return, but eventually you will remember being knocked out and even being surprised that you were capable of being knocked out. You see, you don't really hurt; you only *think* you hurt and you didn't really get hit, you only *think* you got hit, and in the thinking or believing is the creation.

Now; I wish to discuss creation. You are now creating from light and I wish you all to believe that this is true so you will know who you really are. As long as you believe *in* evil you believe that you are evil. This is due in part to the idea that what you create is a direct extension of you. Therefore, if you believe in evil you get to believe that you created evil. You cannot create what is not part of you and you cannot be part of evil because you are God. God is you. You create as God. All that you create is therefore part of God.

Now; I wish that you stop separating God into good and evil. God is love. Love creates as directed. If you correspond, or communicate, with all parts of creation you will learn that everything within creation is within God. God's guts are what you are. I am the stuff that you are made of. There is *nothing* else. How can there be? Nothing exists outside of God. So, *allow* God to be good. Stop *judging* God as evil or bad. This is a lie.

No one – nothing is allowed to exist without consent or reason. There is a reason for everything and it has nothing to do with judgment and separation. Stop believing in something that does not exist. *Only* in your mind does evil exist. You become evil by believing you are evil. If you looked down and saw purple as the color of your skin you may begin to believe that you are purple, but you are not. You are seeing you as purple because you are color-blind. So now of course you may find others who agree with you, but they too are color-blind. Stop trying to justify your belief in right and wrong. Let go of good and bad. *Love is all.* There is nothing else.

In this book I will try to show you how you are love. You are not evil or bad or wrong. You believe that you need rules and commandments to stop you from being bad and I am here to tell you that you can never be bad. It is all an illusion. You are love creating from love without knowledge that what you do is actually very good. It is as though a small child picked up a rock to break a window and decided not to throw it because it is bad or evil to break windows. Dad now arrives on the scene to explain to the child that it's okay to break a window and it's very good to know how strong your throwing arm is. "What about the damage?"– you ask. There is no damage on this plane because it's all an illusion that was built just for this movie, and according to the script, your role or your part calls for you to throw rocks as hard as you can. You may choose to play your part or you may give it up to someone else. Either way it is going to be acted out by someone, because this is the movie everyone agreed to produce in order to entertain the others who are in the audience.

Don't get too wrapped up in who plays what part. It's just a movie. It's not real. It's only fun and play. You began to take it all too seriously and now the director is coming in to say, "Get off your high horse" and stop judging this scene. Play it or leave and let someone else play it. You may not appreciate the role others play, simply because you don't have the entire script and so you don't know why certain components are necessary. Your part is being you and acting as *you* no matter how you judge your ability to create.

Most of you will not understand this, simply because you do not have the capacity for it at this point in time. Therefore, I would like to remind you once again, judgment will keep you down and your goal is to rise above. Rise above all situations simply by seeing through the eyes of love. Leave your dark glasses, which distort the light rays, at home. From now on we wish only to *"see the light."*

God

"Godhood is achieved by each individual in his or her own time. This is not a race; it is simply a course in rising up…."

Once we begin to see how we have been tricked we will allow more light to pour through this dimension. Often it is said that your world is dark indeed. In actuality, your world is quite bright. Before you began to sleep you had the best of both worlds. You knew you were God the creator and you knew all. Now you know little and are unaware of your identity as creator.

This is the time of *change*. You want to wake up and know who you are and in order to wake you must change. Sleep feels good, but too much sleep creates stiffness in your body and sometimes a big headache from all the fluids surrounding the brain. To wake up is to *open*. Open your eyes and see the truth. Open your heart and know you are love. Open your mind and accept you. You are at a point of recreating who you are simply by going forward into you. You will no longer feel the need to be lost. You will feel secure in your findings no matter how you fear looking at what you are. It is not bad nor is it wrong to be human. It is not bad nor is it wrong to be God. Don't judge you for being a co-creator of this galaxy. It is simply your job. It is what you do. Now you have decided to play it a little differently and let go of the pain and hurt that creates dysfunction in your lives.

So; the big question is – how do you know if you have pain and hurt? Very simply, it will rear its head in some fashion and you will know. It's very easy to tell. Do you dislike something and believe it is bad? If so you have pain or hurt attached to this belief, maybe from childhood, maybe from past life. Do you misunderstand people and have confusion relating to their ideas and their beliefs? If so you have confusion in the disguise process. It too comes from pain and hurt. Do you get upset about traffic or people who keep you waiting? If so you have pain and it is showing itself as impatience. Do you tire easily and sleep heavy or too lightly? Either of these are signs of childhood emotional pain or abuse. The light sleeper is aware or "on guard" in order to protect him or herself. The heavy sleeper is trying to escape this problem all together. Do you have health problems? Headaches, sinus problems, backaches, stiff neck, sore muscles when you work them, acne, pimples, diarrhea, constipation, earaches, sight or eye problems, any of these is created by carrying pain within the body. You carry pain by being of the *belief* that you were hurt at one time or another. Let go of your pain.

Do you get edgy and nervous in pressure situations? It is not natural to be nervous. You are told it is, but it is not. It is fear. Fear from a belief in being hurt either physically or emotionally. Most often you fear mental pain. To suggest you are going insane or are mentally disturbed is one of your greatest fears. You are afraid of losing your mind and you are afraid of losing your memory. So you hold on tight. You hold on to everything out of fear of losing you, so now you are so big because *you* includes your identity. And what is your identity? It is everything that you *hold* on to. If you must wear certain clothes or drive a nice car or have certain friends or project a big family image they all become part of you by you holding on to them. Your concern regarding having them in your life or not having them in your life is what keeps you *stuck* to people and stuff. It is your identity. Your ego image is made up of what you choose to hold and what you hold becomes part of you. You are very big at this time.

As you peel off your layers you will feel less restraint and greater freedom. In giving up your hold, you actually receive greater. The less you are holding on to the more light and love that flows through you. You will no longer feel the need to hold to one thing because all things are now yours. You let go and you receive all. It's energy flowing as it was meant to. Think of it as a conveyer belt that contains everything in creation. It constantly winds past your eyes and you pick and choose what you feel you like. The only catch is that when your hands are full you cannot hold the next item. The smart thing to do would be to sample items and then return them so your hands are free to receive the next gift. You are full up and I can't get in. You so desperately want love but your hands are holding on so tightly to your old identity that you have no room for God. Hold God. Do not hold things and people. You are God and yet you have no room, time, or patience for you.

Create a life that is full of love and you will be pain-free. Pain cannot enter where love resides. If you choose to *surrender* it all for love, you are choosing to give up everything you hold dear for God. And who is God? You....

So far it is not your job to discover God. I wish you to know that God is not lost, you are lost. You have always been part of God and you have always known who you are. Now your memory is lost. You have forgotten. Nothing has occurred except amnesia. The only change from knowing your truth was forgetting your truth. It is all simply a matter of remembering and practicing. You may remember by stimulating your mind. Read, learn, understand your mind. You too may learn to communicate with God. Desire will get you God just as desire gets you life. You must begin to wake up and know who you are.

Try to remember that you are more powerful than you know, try to remember that you have been here before. Go into your head. Get into your own mind. Know where you came from. Examine the results and you will *see* how you are actually your own creator. You are the one who does not end. You are the one who knows all, sees all and judges nothing. You are God. God is you. You are the one who slipped into amnesia in order to be different, in order to create, in order to feel. You are God and you have lost your mind, gone crazy, gone into your memory to distort it and change it from its truth.

Once you begin to see how you are indeed God the force, God the creator, God the love, God the light, you will leave you alone and stop judging you for your life. You will begin to know how you are all that exists, and why punish *All That Is* simply for being. Stop punishing yourself and others. Choice is made out of free will. Free will is yours. You allowed free will because you know how nothing is wrong so why make rules? Why else would you stop you from controlling totally? If you were and are God, why on earth would you send us here and say, "you can't do this" and "you can't do that," if you did want us to be free? Why would you begin to grow and procreate and then call it a sin? Why would you begin to learn and feel and then block feeling? Why would you start to learn your full potential as a created being and then block any part of that potential? It must be acted out in order to form properly.

All phases of communication and extortion have been set in play. No one bribes God. I don't care how far back you go and how many lambs you slaughter. No one buys God. It's all a scam. You don't make deals with God because God doesn't care what you create or do not create. Stop promising God you will pay service "if only" he will give you this or that. *You* give you this or that and *you* create what you get or do not get.

Now, the best way to handle creation is to leave it alone and *allow* it to evolve. This is all that I ask. *Leave my creation alone. Allow everything to be and stop judging it.* Is this too much to request? Do you have something against creation and evolution? Why can't you know and use your intuitive ability once again? I suggest that you begin to use your intuition and let go of scheming to get what ego covets. You are on this plane for such a brief moment. Why not leave it in better shape than you find it? Why not love it instead of judging it? Why not *allow* your own evolution without judging it? You are growing and learning, nothing more nothing less, simply growing and learning. Waking and sleeping. Wake up now. This is a new dawn of a new day. You are going to be very happy with your new future.

You have been creating this new future as you go. The more you judge, the heavier your future. The less you judge, the lighter your future. You may determine how well you do by how you judge. Judgment is my last demon to slay. No one ever does wrong. No one ever is evil. Evil does not exist and soon you will *believe* this truth. Stop being afraid of shadows. You are creating fearful situations from a fearful mind. God does not wish to teach fear, God only wishes to be love.

When you have learned how you are teaching fear you will wish to change. When you wish to change, you will. It is simply a matter of using your desire to shift your mentality. No one is bad. Nothing is wrong. Keep it just that simple!

When first I began to channel through this girl I did so at a very low speed. She was open yet incapable of holding my vibration for fear of exploding. She soon became clear and as I took over and worked within her I began to clear her debris. She too clears her debris and takes care to not lose sight of her goal. Her goal is single minded and simple. This girl wants only to return to God. She wishes only to ascend. She is no different than you. She knows it and feels it. You may not know it or feel it consciously.

Since this awakening process is a bit time consuming, it has been somewhat of a problem to keep Liane still as I work within her. I tell you this so you will become aware that I work within each of you. You may not know it consciously, but I do. As you go along you will see your life begin to change. It may look as though your life is falling apart. It is. This is change. When you feel pain you are beginning to heal. The pain is your hurt and dysfunction coming to the surface. You might say that it is a celebration to feel and experience your pain.

As you heal, your pain will seem to float away. Situations, which had been hurtful in the past will no longer hurt or affect you. This is ascension. This is vibrating faster or spinning into the light. You let go of the old pattern of belief that tells you to get hurt and upset. You hold only to your new truth, which is based on good and love and allowing and accepting.

In the past you allowed others to hurt you by allowing yourself to be less than they. This is a time for rising up and knowing your own truth and being less or more than no one. Now you are learning to simply be and do and know that it is okay to say no. It is okay to be alone.

It is okay to want freedom from responsibility. It is okay to run and hide. It is okay to be true to your own self. It is okay to know what you want and go for it. It is okay to not want anything and not do anything. Everything is okay. Life is okay. Death is okay. Judgment is heavy. Acceptance is light. Some wish light. Some wish dark. Let it all be okay. I will teach you how to see both sides and I will tell you what you prefer from a spiritual point of view. However, you are not viewing from spirit, so you may opt for other or opposing choices. This too is okay. All is okay. Free will is just that – *free*dom to choose.

Therefore; when I tell you that you must stop judgment in order to ascend it is true, but you may not wish to *accept* this truth or you may not wish to be *light* at this time. You may wish to continue to sleep. This too is okay! You may wish to continue to layer yourself in debris and density. This too is okay. You may wish to remain in the material plane and never leave. You always get what you *desire.* Desire God and you get God. Desire heaven and you get heaven. Desire pain and you get pain. Desire love and you get love. So why don't you have love? You say you know what you want, but do you really? Can you really know what you desire when you do not even know who you are or what makes you tick?

I once told you that you are destructive and that you tick like a bomb waiting to go off. You are and you do. None of you is *in* spirit. You are all in matter and you are so thick with it that you have lost the true essence of your own being. I highly suggest you get in touch with your own identity. You may begin by communicating directly with your soul. Talk to the voices in your head. Talk to the voice in your heart. Begin to know you. Get reconnected with your own self. Stop running away from who and what you are. You are good. Go back *into* you and own you. You may ascend just by accepting who you are, but if you never look at who you are, how can you know you?

You are so magnificent and yet you believe you are no more than dirt. You are actually like a bright star who fell out of the heavens and now is covered with dirt and rust from laying in the foulness that is beginning to decay this world. However, if you will just look – that's all you have to do is look at yourself – you can clean and rebuild your own brightness. You have the ability within you to stop this decay. You came here self-sufficient and very capable of shining through all of this dirt and debris. This is the *illusion* of matter. It is not real. You are still a bright shiny star. You are buried because you bought into this illusion. Let go of this illusion and let go of this layer that keeps you dull.

You will begin to shine by letting your light pour forth. You will know when this occurs because you will feel very, very good. You will accept at every turn and you will judge nothing and you will hold on to nothing. When you have learned to be fluid, you will have *unstuck* yourself from this plane. "To have or not to have, that is the question." The answer to this dilemma is "have it all by letting it all go." You may own; you may buy; you may give birth to, but do not covet. Do not hold to. Do not stick to. Allow total freedom. Act as though everything you have is being auctioned off tomorrow to pay bills. Then you may have it without desire or attachment to it. You will learn the true meaning of "light" and "freedom" and "flowing."

You have a great deal to learn and you have a great universal mind to explore. It is all within you. I am within you. I am within Liane. I encourage you all to communicate with me. I am the universal mind – the Akashic Records – the infinite knowledge and wisdom of all experience. For the time and place and level that you are, I give what you are *willing* to accept at this time. There is so vast a library of information within you that you too could channel books forever. You only need tap that source. Do your enemas. Get the blocks out of your body. Everything is within. Look within! Clean within! Reside within! Love is within….

When you begin to clear away the debris that exists within you, you will become clear. You will have cleaned your body, your mind and your spirit. You are dusty and rusty but this is easily fixed. You forgot, now you're being told to remember. You cannot take long because you are on a schedule. You are being pulled by energy to wake up and clean up and get on with this business of being God.

You are not alone and you are not stuck without consent. Give permission to rise up and you rise up. Give permission to clear and you clear. Give permission to know and you know. There are many tricks you have used to keep you under. You have drugged yourself to the extent that you are hallucinating and *reacting* to those hallucinations. I will guide you through these hallucinations to your true identity. Just ask. Ask to know the truth. There are many affirmations that will assist you in awakening. Some of you are easily assisted, others take a little longer. Do not consider your leadership as good or bad. Do not consider your lateness in awakening as good or bad. No competition please. You are simply waking up and each of you has his or her own way. Live within you, do not desire to live within another.

When you wake up you will know how you have power and how you create your own life. When you wake up you will *feel* how you create a situation to win or lose. It is best to give up this game of winning in order to let go of losing. There are no winners therefore there can be no losers. There is always an opposite action that creates problems for you. The way to see this differently is to make everything okay – no big deal. Winning is just okay. Losing is just okay. None of it really matters. This will de-power low self-esteem and give everyone hope. The winner is constantly afraid of falling from his position of winning and the loser is obsessed with achieving some kind of recognition and gets resentful. Let everyone just be. No more trophies please. All this nonsense is simply separation.

I know you wish to do good by awarding your gifted parts, but you are so unconscious that you are awarding for what you do not understand. Once you give an award you then monitor to make certain your deserving achiever does not fall from grace or does not dishonor his or her award status. Let it all go. If you wish to choose those who stand out in *your* eyes, I suggest you choose everyone involved to receive an award. Your eyes do not know what is successful (or achievement) because your eyes are not clear. Make everyone deserving of every award because you are singling out situations and events that may not be truth. Example: You give scholarships in your schools for learning, but in actuality what you are teaching are lies. It is only the illusion that you teach and you give awards for those who learn the lie the best. Don't you think this is a little silly? Wouldn't it be better to give awards to those who do not learn? Those who refuse to take on the lie or *illusion* of this plane. You think about this for awhile while I communicate with my pen.

This is not a good time to be unfair with who you are. You came here to experience and to feel emotion. You are part of a very big plan and this very big plan *allows* for all to occur. Most of you are very concerned in world issues. You believe that you must get everyone to do everything the *right way* in order to save your world. This is not true. Your world is changing and change is good. So; how can you stand by and allow others to chop down trees and rape this planet of her resources? Just as I have explained that you do not die ever, I will explain that she (earth) does not die ever. How can earth die when she is simply a reflection of you?

You may help her and stop harming her by helping you and not harming you. She is the womb. She nurtures and she supports. She is life. She is meant to be love. You support, you nurture; you are life. When you begin to love and accept you without judgment, you will be loving, and accepting Mother Earth and your neighbors without judgment. It cannot occur any other way. All is you and you are all. Hold on to nothing – let go of all. You will learn how you are the earth by learning who you are. Each reflection is based on its master. You are the master thought. You have projected out into billions but only one thought was originally projected. You are accountable for all other projections.

So; doesn't it stand to reason that when you love you, you love every part of you? And in loving, you are shedding light on, and in shedding light on, you are nurturing and supporting. If you ache inside because your planet aches, then I suggest you begin to look at your own personal pain and see how it is that you are reflecting so much pain into your world. Everything is connected to everything else. Heal you and you heal all. You have no *idea* how powerful you are. Please begin to see this idea clearly. It is all up to you. You are God. You create; you destroy. If you can but love your own self you can heal this entire world. Focus on you. Do not waste your time focusing on your reflection.

If a mirror shows a crooked tie you do not clean

off the mirror, you simply straighten your tie and the image or reflection is automatically changed. It is that simple. It is all a matter of coming back to center and no longer chasing shadows or reflections. Leave everyone else alone. Go your own way and heal your own heart. You will not hurt when you love you. You will not hurt when you focus on you and not on others. Stop your pain and your frustration by focusing only on you and healing you. Get your pain to the surface so you may unjudge it. You will feel better. I will feel better. And this planet will feel better. It may take you some time but time does not exist and you are here for this reason only. You came to bring love to this plane. You came to love. Love is not holding hands and kissing. Love is not attachment to others. Love is not digging in deeper in matter. *Love is accepting you as God.*

It is so simple. When you *accept* that this is all *you* and that you may heal all by healing you, you will be God by consent. You will be love by consent. You already are, but you do not accept it. If you did you would not struggle to fix others or your planet. If you accepted your Godhood you would simply fix you, heal you. You are standing on the threshold of understanding and soon you will begin to acknowledge and accept who you are. As long as you deny your Godhood, you deny love. Love does not die, however love denied fades and leaves. It will always find a place to present itself where it will be accepted. Accept love and it is yours. You too may become God simply by accepting God (love).

Once in a very great while you begin to listen. You show signs of knowing and changing. After you learn who and what you are, you will highly approve of my teaching techniques. You will begin to see how I have led you simply and gently *into* you. You need not stay *in* you once you have gone within to discover what is there. Just knowing who and what you are is enough to raise you up.

After you have learned your truth you will begin to rise automatically. Simply knowing what makes you tick allows you to stop ticking. When you see how you are programmed and sending out signals to others based on this past programming, you will begin to know how to change your programming into something positive. Everything that you have taught yourself to believe can be untaught. Every judgment and adversity can be changed into good. You may not wish to see it as good right away, but with time you will see its benefits. Everything has two sides. It is positive and negative at the same time.

Now; what you have taught yourself to do on this plane is to see the negative because you are not all here. You are still growing as God and literally coming into yourselves. In the beginning you saw negative and now you are going to switch and see positive. Evil is not evil unless you *choose* to see the negative. Love is not love unless you chose to see the positive. The opposite of love is hate. If you do not see *everything* as love you are looking at its *opposite* to some degree. Do not carry hate. This point of view will kill you.

So; if you begin to know that negative and positive are the exact same energy, you will begin to accept yourself for having committed what you call negative acts. No matter how you judge hate, it is only the opposite end of love. Draw a circle and put a line through it. You now have what looks like a pie cut in half. Write the word "love" at one end of this line and the word "hate" at the opposite end. Now make another line (or cut) through your pie, so you have four pieces of pie. Now write the word "guilty" at one end of this new line and the word "innocent" at the other end. At what point does innocence become guilt? Do you see how this works? No one is innocent or guilty. The energy runs both ways and *cancels* out the entire idea of polarities. Polarities do not exist. It is one in the same thing. You may create negative or positive. It's your choice.

The reason you chose negative is because you have been taught to fear. You have been taught to *focus* on worry and to protect yourself from pain, death, injury, etc. *You* create these as negative by calling them negative. I will now give you an example: Say you have overcome your fear of death to the extent that you believe it will be quite enjoyable. You will get to leave your body and you will get to go to the light. You may have read a great deal about after death experience and learned that the majority of those who die for brief moments and see the light and love of God do not wish to return to life. So, you may have concluded that this peace and joy that they experience must feel very good indeed. This makes you question your fear of death. You now believe it to be a very loving experience. How do you relate this to your friends? You simply tell them to picture an island where love and truth prevails. This may be the same island you read about in Book Seven where parents teach their children about the goodness of sex.

So; you are now living on this island and your parents and grandparents have always told you about this wonderful experience you may someday wish to know. They say it is quite exalting and very, very beautiful. They have taught you, since early childhood, how you may transform your beliefs by taking part in this life/death experience. Your village, of course, is quite civilized and love is the predominant factor in all your life teachings. So, the elders organize a situation whereby one of the village members may experience this thing called death, where you feel peace and joy and are told your meaning in this particular life. Do you volunteer or are you afraid? It is easy to see how your training has taught you to fear instead of love or accept. Once you learn how to love, you will be volunteering for anything that feels good, and most things will feel good because you will be seeing good instead of bad. You will see through the eyes of God instead of evil.

Yes! I know you have a long way to go. But remember, it starts with your first step and then another and yet another. It will build and grow faster with each step you take. It is rather like a rescue mission. You are all being rescued from this crash, and those who can walk on their own go home first. Those who are cripple will be carried out, and some of those who are trapped and traumatized by fear will need lots of love and reassurance before we can even carry them out. You who have walked out may even return to assist the rest. This is ascension. This is the "A" Team walking toward the light as the light moves in to rescue.

So far it is best to only show you what you can willingly handle. You would become upset if you knew your true heritage. You have hidden from your truth for so long that it would feel too oppressive to show you all that you have chosen. You will soon see how what you have chosen will look even better through the eyes of love.

When you hide off parts of yourself it is due to fear and judgment. So; how long have you played this game of hiding you from you? It all started as you began to judge you for not being best or as good as you judged others. The only problem with this theory of yours is that you judged according to mishap. As long as you thought for a brief moment that something was greater or better than something else, it became hidden in some way. It was now "put down" in your opinion and was judged as 'not' good or 'not' as good. Each time something was "put down" as 'not' good and judged as so by you, you went down with this "put down" because it is all you.

So; judge it as bad and you go down a notch with it.

This is your yardstick to measure how deeply embedded you are. You are only as far down as you have judged. Thus we have the statement – "judge not lest ye be judged." With every judgment call, you send you a little lower and you put greater distance between you and God. You are not to judge you any longer. Leave you be and allow you to create whatever you choose. If you do not get good scores on a test that is so simple your dog could take it and pass it easily, do not judge you. Know that you are who you are and how you are for a reason. If you feel that you cannot catch up with the crowd and current trends, it is okay. Not all current trends go to a light. Some even march deeper into matter.

So; I highly suggest that you follow your own beat, and march to your own tune and do not be afraid to be different. Break away from the pack and follow your own guidance to the light. Do things that are good and loving to your own self. Do not get caught up in the trap of following like a lamb to slaughter. Most of your social and economic structure is based on such tradition. You must follow certain rules, and dress a certain way, and marry, and have a family, and be proud of your family, and be proud of your job and your status. This is old programming. Now it is okay to say, "I do not want to be married," or "I do not want wealth," or "I do not want to pay taxes," or "I do not want a government telling me what to do."

You have many, many, many options. But you are so restricted by your fear that you keep what you do not want. In the same way that you stay with a mate who is not kind to you, you stay with a system that is not kind to you.

You are afraid to stand up to your mate because you do not wish to be alone and unloved. You are afraid to stand up to your government because you think you need them to protect you. You are again afraid of being alone and without help or protection. You do not need a mate nor do you need a government to rule over you. You will learn in the very near future that all of creation is meant to be a gift. So, why select one of creation's gifts if it does not feel good to you.

You may wish to know that some people desire pain because pain is an old friend to them, so they will choose gifts that bring pain. If you are one of those who find comfort in pain because you were raised with a certain amount of pain, I do suggest you begin to change this programming by telling yourself repeatedly, "I deserve love, I am love; I deserve joy, I am joy. I deserve peace, I am peace."

Old cycles and old programs can be broken; it is simply a matter of no longer desiring pain and hurt. When you know you have drawn it like an old friend, you can make the choice to draw something more to your liking. If you deny that you draw it, or spend all your time and energy getting comfortable with it, you will 'not' *see* that you are never meant to be less than happy with all your choices. There is no "grin and bear it." There is only love, so always choose love for yourself. See how you create for yourself by seeing how you hurt yourself. It is not your job to punish you, nor is it your job to put you in a hurtful situation. As long as you love you, you will give you only loving situations.

You are not meant to be in pain ever. Let go of your hold on pain so it can move to its right place. You do not belong in pain you belong in love. You get love by learning that love is acceptance. Accept you; all parts of you, then we can begin to look at the parts that crave pain and heal them. Your definition of pain may even be love. Many of you believe that "love equals pain," so you avoid love and embrace pain without even knowing that you do.

---

*I*t is not often that you and I talk. Why do you think that is? Why do you believe it is not good to *allow* God to speak to you? You have wanted to communicate for over two thousand years and yet you have done little to actually get this communication going. Picture this: You have just built a giant satellite dish to assist you in communication with God. As you reach the point of completion, the wind blows through and knocks over your satellite dish. Now you have no way to communicate with God. So you give up. Just at that moment, five thousand miles away, someone is communicating with God without any fuss or bother. That someone, simply uses his hand to write information that seems to come from inside. And how does he know that this is God? Trust. Trust that God resides inside each of you.

So; the next time you complain about God never

getting in touch with you, I suggest you sit down and let or allow God to write. The enemas will assist in getting enough biological debris out of your system so that you too may write for God. Don't give up. Try often and allow whatever is to occur to be good. You each have the ability to communicate with me. Maybe it will take some time, maybe it won't. It is not wrong to want to communicate with God and it is not wrong to channel. You *are* simply a channel for God so why not act like it?

Now; I wish to discuss this problem you have with your body. It is no more an instrument for God than I am an instrument for you. You are taught that your body belongs to God and you have no say over it. Your body belongs to you and you may do whatever you like with it. If you kill it, God does not die. If you live in it, you share it with God only on invitation. A body may be inhabited with a soul or uninhabited. You are not all *in* body. Some of you guide from without and yes! This is possible. One way in which to bring light into your body is to channel it in. Think of light. Light will follow light, and thought is energy which moves through your body. So, fill your body with light by constantly asking to be light. Allow God to enter.

If you have a soul in house I can work with your soul. If your soul is waiting to be born I can assist. You are all in a state of birthing. You are being born of the light and are all at various stages of this birth. Now, don't freak out here and run out to profess to the world that some of you have no soul. You each are soul. You each don't necessarily live in body. This should give you pause for a moment.

Now, when you begin to communicate with God, you will know that it is you, for *you* are God. So, as you begin to write for God you will feel like it is coming from you or like you are doing it. And of course, some part of you is. Do not worry. Do not give up. It will become apparent at some point in your communication that some part of you gives answers a little differently than this "personality you" would give. As you allow this information to write through you, it will grow in depth and in volume. Practice makes perfect. Get in touch with you. Stop running off to psychics and astrologers and sit down and give yourself your own answers. You are the living mind of God so stop pretending that you have no way of entering or taping into your own truth.

It is all here, right inside of you. You have the best source of all information sitting *in* you and yet you turn to everyone else for your answers. Learn to tap into you; tap into God. You are the living memory of God and it only takes the *will* to discover and the energy to sit and write, or even sit and listen if you care to communicate telepathically. You *are* the mind of God. You are the information you so desperately seek. You already have what you desire to make you God. Look at you. Look in you. You are everything and you do not know it.

One of these days you will see clearly how all this works, and then you will be very thankful that you were taught early on to do enema and clean out the storehouse of built-up debris that blocks the flow of life force, which is of course, God. So; you want God in you – then let him in. You want light in you – then let it in. You want to talk with God – then, do it!

*When I first began to write through this woman, it was very hard. She had no idea (and still doesn't) how she was doing this. She frightened herself on several occasions and she even began to promise she would not channel again. There are many parts of you who wish to communicate with you and they will do so in one way or another. Most of what you will see will be very difficult to comprehend unless you know to stay calm and always have faith. They (those you communicate with) will simply be expressing from where they are. You see, some parts of you are under-developed and I suggest that you begin to communicate with all parts in order to assist you in your own growth.

So, if you find yourself communicating with some part of you who expresses evil, begin to ask why it is still dark and if it wishes to go to the light. Make it your friend by allowing it to choose between light or dark. If it still wishes to stay undercover and not move forward to the light I suggest you allow it to. It is up to each part of you as to whether or not it goes to the light. It will always give you correct information if it is light. This is not true of the dark. When you channel the darkness do not be afraid. It is simply part of you that is hurt and buried. You will begin to understand more fully as you move closer to the light. Often this movement toward the light creates the movement of darkness to the surface.

If you channel evil, know that it is some part of you talking back to you. Do not freak out as my pen did. Stay calm and either communicate or don't communicate. It is up to you. I suggest that whenever possible you see what you are really doing by allowing all energy to pass and by allowing all energy to communicate. It is best to receive information from all parts of you. Even the dark parts. Do not be afraid – they will not take over. Surround yourself with love and light and allow communication to take place.

You will find that even big bad voices will respond to love and understanding. It is all pain that is buried in you and at times it is rage. Rage may appear as a huge monster who has control of you, but you will learn that in bringing your rage to the surface you will be able to confront it and to heal it. Everything is energy and everything moves through you and around you. You will see how you create greater darkness by your rage and anger. This darkness is in you and may frighten you with its force. Do not be afraid.

In the beginning Liane tried to hide from her voices. She could not hide because they were part of her. She heard anger and rage appear as an evil voice who even said he was not light. She eventually talked to this evil voice and as she communicated she learned that this voice had a conscience. This voice was trying to frighten her. It was her memory of a very bad deed that she had suppressed, and now that memory was coming up at her in the only way it knew how.

As Liane talked with this voice asking if it knew of God and love, it became more frightened because it thought God its enemy. After all, where was God or love in the middle of these terrible acts that were perpetrated against a little girl? She was only five and had no one to turn to. So how could God or love be anything good? The one who hurt her was suppose to love her. So love must be painful and evil. And God – this wonderful father in heaven who is suppose to watch over us – where was he in the middle of her shame? Why didn't he watch over and protect? What good is he? "I hate God" is the response you may receive from the dark side of you, so do not let it frighten you.

Evil is no more evil than God is. It is simply energy that is confused and does not understand. Liane communicated with her evil voice until it understood there was hope and he (the big bad voice) agreed to work with her soul in coming to the light. Fear begets fear. Love begets love and communication begets communication. Talk to you. Talk to God.

Now is a very good time to begin to know who you are. You have been very quiet about your own identity and you have been very well protected from discovery. Mostly I wish you to become all that you were meant to be.

You have been in a state of unconsciousness for a very long time and now it is your time to become conscious and aware. Most of what you experience on this plane has to do with little other than gestation at this time.

You slumber. You await the time of awakening and that time is at hand. As you begin to wake up you begin to know more without knowing how you know. The most difficult process will be *trusting.* You have been unaware for so long that trusting may be difficult within your first waking moments. As you begin to flow with the knowledge and awareness of who you are, you will become different than your current state of life. You will change.

You will begin to see life differently and you will begin to *know* how life truly works. This will create calm. This calmness will be seen in you as a lack of emotional stress regarding life as you now know it. Put very simply, you will not "care" so much and you will not allow concern to take over your life. Out of this lack of emotional concern will come "peace" this peace is eternal and is waiting for you to step into it. It is quite simple to do. Calm down and *watch.* Do not judge.

This is your lesson for today. I wish you to stay calm and observe. Know that creation is perfect as it is and simply observe everything that occurs today. A good way to deal with this lesson is to know that everything is in perfect synchronicity. Just because you are unaware of the meaning of life does not mean that life has no meaning.

Whenever you wish to create, you often do not use your power. You often use your programming. You are intelligence and yet you do not fully appreciate your intelligence nor do you know how to use it. You believe you are intelligent and yet you believe you are a victim. How can you be intelligent life who makes its own choices for good reason if you believe in victim hood?

To be a victim is to give power to someone else. If you are a victim of childhood trauma it is because you chose it. You knew what circumstances would be in play and you wanted to experience without thought of pain. You often choose situations that are difficult, only because they cause greater stretching of the imagination. Greater stretching creates greater growth. If you are in a situation that is not good it is because you chose it. This is true even if you are the child. You agreed, for whatever reason, to enter into a situation that looks from your point of view to be painful and harmful. From a point of view outside of this dimension it is neither painful nor harmful. It simply is an experience without any judgment of good or bad.

So; in order to have a bad experience it must be *judged* as bad. In order to have pain you must judge something as painful. It is not necessarily a painful situation for everyone because some of you create pain easily and some of you take more time to make something painful. It is all the same thing. Some may feel pain from it and some may not. So; is it painful or is it in the mind that sees it as painful? If two people get hit with a small rock and one yells "ouch" while the other doesn't even feel the rock hit, what is painful? Is hitting someone with a rock painful or is the pain stored already in each individual body? And if this pain is already stored in each individual body, how did it get there?

So, if you have pain but your friend does not (when you are each hit with a rock) are you both victims or is just the one who feels the pain a victim? How far can this go? If you are a robot and feel nothing then you may not be valued for your life, since you appear to not have life. If you have life you have pain and are vulnerable right...? Wrong! If you have life you are life. Life is ongoing without regard for feelings or pain or what you call death. Life goes on. Nothing stops life.

Now; when you are hit by your rock, it is a situation by which you might *explore* yourself and find out what makes you tick. You are this created life, and part of you is so powerful it can force you to look at who and what you are by getting you to ask that very famous question, "Why me?" You are not here to explore the universe; you are here to explore you. You are not here to throw rocks at one another, but if being hit by a rock will help wake you up, you will most likely *agree* to be hit by a rock. Why? Because the bigger part of you knows the truth. "The truth shall set you free!" Know your own truth.

Get hurt if you must, but it is not necessary. You need not push yourself to such extremes. The pain is not outside of you. The pain is not in the rock and the pain is not in the thrower of the rock. The pain is in you. You create pain by believing in pain. You now have thousands of lifetimes of pain to clear. This is why you are a sick society with huge doctor bills. You are all dying on the inside by your own thoughts and beliefs. Let go of judgment. This will be your first step in releasing your hold on pain.

*F*or such a long time you have been without help because you were meant to rise to a certain level with your own resources. You were allowed to float free and to submerge whenever you felt the need. It is no longer necessary for you to stay submerged. You are being pulled up out of this area of creation.

Once you learn the difference between love and war you will no longer wish to entertain war. Most of you have at one time or another been put to the test where war is concerned. You simply engage in battle and scream and yell or hit and I don't know why you choose this sort of competition. Anyway, you will grow out of this need to scream at the top of your lungs and this need to hit or strike back. You will embrace peace. You will "turn the other cheek" – which by the way, does not mean let them strike your other cheek. It simply means, let them do what they want, but you're not going to be any part of it. You will turn and walk away. Turn your other cheek is a way of saying, "turn around and leave." Words have changed a great deal and I'm certain Jesus would be most upset to know how literally most of you have *used* his words against one another.

You are not to push the teachings of old writings at anyone until you discover their true intent. This has not been good for you and you have fought far too many wars over this one. You still fight over religion and who has the correct meaning of life. You are all quite silly you know? So, as long as you are in this class studying God's books you will make peace not war. You make peace by not engaging in war. You do not engage in war by walking away, or by speaking calmly and peacefully on any subject.

I know that protest creates change and helps you get what you think is important for this planet. I wish you to know that fighting is fighting, and yelling and screaming to get your way is fighting. You will find that the way to heal your inner self is to stay calm and to leave everyone else alone. Let the world work without your energy input. That is what you do each time that you get *involved.* You put energy into something else. I wish you to keep your energy in order to heal.

If you do not wish to heal and ascend at this time you may continue to do battle or to put your energy into fighting for your right. Just know that when you fight for something it becomes part of you, and now I have more difficulty bringing you up and out of everything that you have submerged yourself into. "Flow." Let life move in and around you. Do not control life. Do not bend it to your will. We are in a healing, peaceful mode. We are not in our power and control mode.

So, if you wish to stay flexible and peaceful do not engage in any form of aggressiveness. No pushing, shoving, shouting, name calling or hitting please. This will save all of your healing energy for *your* healing.

I wish to discuss pain as seen from other levels. Pain does not exist and is only an excuse to be helped or receive attention. Often when you go to war you do so with the *intent* to get hurt. You, of course, do not consciously know that you do. In the same way that some are hurt (on purpose) on the battlefield, some are hurt on the battlefields right here at home. *Intent* has a great deal to do with pain and injury. Intent says that pain will give way to sympathy and intent also says that pain will increase concern. Some of you actually *believe* that you will not receive enough attention for your cause until a few injuries occur. So, intent plays a very big role in your lives at this time. Not only do you have a desire to harm others, you have a desire to harm yourself. Did you ever wonder why so many of you are drinking and smoking even though it kills you? You do not care! You are here and you want to harm you in some way for something you have done that you judged as bad.

How many of you freak out over sending your child to school when you have just been told a child in class has AIDS? How many of you avoid AIDS victims and would not feed them at your own table? This is paranoia. You are all dying. You are killing yourself just as readily and as surely as anyone who is dying of AIDS. Stop yelling about safe sex. Until you take that cigarette out of your hands and that bottle of booze out of your mouth, you too are having unprotected or unsafe sex. You simply have *chosen* a slower way to kill yourself. So, if you can have your own personal deathtrap, so can they. Leave them alone. Leave everyone alone to do it their way. If you do not believe that each puff you take and each drink you take is a step closer to pain and injury to your vital organs you are a very foolish dreamer.

Now, when I first began to write these books I did not reprimand you so much, but now you are older and *wiser*. Aren't you?

So far we have covered a great deal of information in this series of books. It is best to allow all information to be digested gradually and to not form *solid* beliefs around such information. This is due to the fact that all is constantly fluid and all is constantly changing. So, as you go along I wish you to remember that no one has the last word on anything because there is no last word.

As you begin to grow in acceptance I will be able to give greater depth of understanding to what you now know or have read. As you grow in understanding, you will grow in spirit. Most often it is not you who is to be taught, often it is other parts of you and therefore your personal understanding is not the goal. Your understanding has a great deal to do with your flexibility. You will find that it is not only understanding that is lacking as you read new material concerning your true identity, it is also a level of awareness and perceptibility. You are capable of perceiving all if you will only open to receive all.

As you grow in harmony and balance you will begin to accept more readily what God wants for his children. What God wants for his children is of the highest possible glory. They may be content for now; however there will come a time of great awakening when each of you will *desire* only the truth with no camouflage. It is often difficult to find the truth when you live in a three dimensional world. These dimensions in themselves are a lie or an illusion. The three dimensional world is not three dimensional at all. You are living in a multi-dimensional world and you choose to see only three sides. Allow yourself to see it all. There is so much that you are shutting out, that you are hiding from you. When you begin to open up you will begin to allow all that you wish to draw to you. Right now you may wish for, but you block this wishing by not allowing.

All phases of life are meant to be experienced, but not taken seriously. I know this is difficult for those who feel overburdened and in pain. You are in a hole and see no way out. I want you to look around. There is always a way out. Always! Not always will you *accept* this way out, but please *accept* that it is possible. You limit yourself only by your rules and your fears. You will allow yourself out when you are ready. I cannot interfere if you do not request it.

You are in charge only because you fear *allowing* God to be in charge. This is why I have control over the life of my pen. Liane gave her free will choices over to me. She allows me to run her life.

She has landed in situations that were not and still are not comfortable for her. This is my doing. I create for her. So; why would a loving God make a child so uncomfortable? It is what is necessary to *release* her pain created by her guilt. She believes, in the deepest part of her, that she committed a giant evil sin as a little girl. She let someone have sex with her and her mind cannot handle this. So she shut her mind off and created amnesia. Then she forgot and went on about her life. The interesting part in all this is that she did not forget. Only her conscious personality forgot. The unconscious mind knows. The unconscious or subconscious mind is in the cells. Every cell of every body contains memory and belief and judgment.

So now she has forgotten her big bad sin, only her body knows what she did and her guilt begins to eat her alive. Now, at a young age of thirty she begins to have health problems, and shortly after she is hit by a falling window. Accidents are common with those of you who wish to punish yourselves. If you are always hurting yourself it is not really accidental, as accidents don't really exist. So; as Liane creates more and more pain to ease her guilt as she grows, she begins to die a little inside. This is where God comes in. She was ready for change to the extent that she would give her body over to God without a bargain in the deal for herself. She did not ask for a deal as often you do. She asked for nothing in return. She simply stated that she was not doing a good job of this life and was no longer happy. She simply wanted God to take over and she offered to do whatever God wanted; not what she wanted.

Now she has what she asked for. God writes his books through her hand, and God puts her in a place that will assist her in clearing and releasing all pain and judgment held against herself for her sins. She is not always happy, but she is getting there. She is not always light, but she is getting there; she is not always love, but she is getting there. She is on her way to peace and joy. It took a little while to clear away the cobwebs and to force her to release her grip on the belief that she did something seriously wrong, but now she knows on all levels and in the knowing she is healing.

You too hold judgment against you for past discretions. Let it all go. It doesn't matter what you did. It is not important. If you wish to know how harshly you are judging you and killing you from the inside out, you may tell by how you see others. If you judge certain acts harshly you will most certainly be judging you harshly. The outside world is simply a reflection of what you are doing on the inside of you.

When you become light vibration you will no longer believe in fear. Your body will no longer rule. Body now rules because body carries mind in its cellular structure. You, do not belong to body, you belong to spirit. As body begins to let go of its hold on memory you will feel confused. You will want to do certain things, but you may not have the get-up-and-go to actually function as your will dictates. This is simply spirit taking over. Often it is a matter of spirit moving in and allowing you to stop. Stop rushing about, stop pushing yourself and stop pushing at life.

So now we have spirit taking over and you are losing ground quickly. Spirit will teach you that it is okay to let go. It is okay to make crazy decisions. It is okay to trust that God is taking care of you. It is okay to unlock your doors. It is okay to love and trust. These, of course, are all crazy ideas in your current world. I mean, everyone knows you must have locks on all your doors and never, ever speak to strangers, and worst of all, don't ever trust anyone because you never know who might be a serial killer. So you spend your life hiding from life and this too will change. For now it is starting gradually, but it will change.

You, my dear sweet children are going to become free spirit. You will not care what happens to you, because you will have clear knowledge that if you are hurt you will not hold it and if you are killed you will simply see God – no big trauma; no big deal. This belief will free you. You will know that you are safe and in a win/win situation. The knowing creates winning. You will be free of fear of death.

Fear of harm will not exist. You will be free.

When you begin to access your greatest potential, you will be accessing spirit. You are body, mind and spirit. You readily use your mind; you even use your body. You, however, have no idea as to how to operate your spirit. Why do you think that is? How can you be something and not know how it operates, or to put it better, how *you* operate? How is it that you have total ignorance as to how spirit operates? How is it that you have no way of communicating with part of you? How is it that you don't have the curiosity to discover how your own body works or why it breaks down? You leave it to science or medicine to tell you what to do with your own private body. How is it that you don't know how to use your mind other than to figure out arithmetic or computers?

Only a few humans have been even remotely concerned with these issues. You use everything outside of you to distract you. Have you ever seen a slide projector showing pictures on a giant screen? Well, this is what you are. You project images and then you spend all of your time and taxpaying money to study these images. Why not spend money to study the depth of *human* resources and leave the outer resources for later. You begin to see how a tree has grown and developed by looking at its layers or rings. See how humanity has developed by looking at your layers.

It is not wrong to investigate or search for answers outside of yourself, but it is a waste of time, for all of your answers are within. "The kingdom of God is within you," not outside on the projected image. Study you. You are the most valuable specimen you will ever study. Know who you are. Do not be afraid to look at your own self and to heal your own personal pain. In the healing of you, will come the healing of this entire universe. Don't bother to heal the projected image. It is not sick. The sender is sick. The projector needs adjustment.

When you begin to realize that you are all that there is you will begin to take better care of you. You will begin to see how it does not matter what goes on around you, because what goes on around you is simply a reflection of what is in you. You will begin to go within and you will begin to accept yourself and all that you have ever done. In this acceptance process will come the acceptance of yourself and all that you create. This will allow you to accept all that is, and yourself as the creator of all that is. This will lead to letting it be okay for creation to exist as it is, and will lead to allowing you to be okay as is. This will lead to you being okay without judgment against you. And without any judgment against you, you become a "free" being. It's just like in *your* world. If no one presses charges against you, you are never tried and convicted. You are never sentenced or given a penance.

So; I suggest you all begin to open your jails and set yourselves free. You did nothing wrong. You do not need to suffer for your sins. You are not bad. You are not guilty. You are love and light. You do not need to be in pain. You do not need to be punished. Let it all go. You are good, you are not evil. You are God.

*W*henever you begin to move more rapidly you begin to shoot through time and space. All movement is connected to growth and stimulation. As you move you begin to see new sights. This too is a sign of growth. New sights create greater stimulation and greater stimulation is what you like. Stimulation is not bad. Stimulation is simply friction, which you use to ignite you. However; if your goal is peace, you will wish to slow down or stop stimulation, as friction is war.

The only time that friction is not war is when it is in the form of stimuli for your cells. Stimuli for your cells could be anything from drugs to caffeine. It is often said that drugs put you to sleep and this is quite true. Alcohol is quite a stimulant and too much of it forces you to pass out.

Nicotine is also a stimulant and quite a powerful one. It is also quite deadly for your cells. Alcohol is deadly to your entire blood system as well as the cells and neurons surrounding brain tissue.

When you begin to consume large doses of stimuli, you begin to create friction or war *within* you. Your cells and nerve endings literally begin to fight to survive. You are killing you off one cell at a time and your cells are reproducing as fast as they can until they become exhausted and begin to give up. At the point of giving up is when the immune system begins to shut down. It no longer can handle the input of friction or the war you created inside of you, so it shuts off and you have no protection from other disorders that affect the body and the mind.

If you wish to stimulate yourself, read a good book or go for a walk in the woods. You are killing you by stimulating your senses to the point of destruction to your own cells. Your cells must be healed in order to transform to the light. All parts of you transform, and the longer it takes you to heal the slower your rise or ascension. Start now. Give your body a break. No more friction or stimuli please. It is killing you.

When you begin to wake up, you will feel as though you are seeing everything differently. You may begin to move to a new area and you may begin to change who you are by letting go of old attachments. These attachments may be to objects, to ideas, or even to people. As you begin your awakening process, it is most important to *allow* and *accept* your new behavior. You are simply coming alive. You are waking up and moving into position to be in your right place. There is no wrong place; however there is a way of "becoming" without being hurt. If you are on your path and you ask God to be put in your right place, you are simply asking God to show you how to get to that doorway. God will always assist you if you are serious in your request. You will always be moved to your right place or to the area of space and time that will assist you most in your evolution.

Do not be afraid to move to your right place. Do not be afraid to do God's work. Do not be afraid to wake up. Do not be afraid of the light. God's ways are not always man's ways. God's ways often have little to do with logic and a great deal to do with love of self. Love of self supersedes all else. You do not put others before you as you are all others and to put everyone ahead of you is to say that all others are not equal to you. You must learn to love you, for you are God. The love of God is being born right inside of you. Your entire kingdom is within you. All the knowledge and information that is stored in the mind of God is in you.

How do you think Liane writes all of this? It is within as well as without. The only difference between within and without is that the projection is what you see without. The outside world is a projection of the inner realms. What do you think of that? Look at all that you have to discover regarding you. You, my dear sweet child of God are everything. You are limitless and you create the very existence that you live in. If you do not like what you see, simply *shift* your perception.

You will find that you are very, very vast indeed. And you will find that you no longer wish to be alone or separated from you. You are going to unite within your own beingness and you will have the most wonderful relationship with you. All relationships lead to oneness. Your search for someone to love is simply a reflection of how you are searching for yourself to love. You are God and yet you search for God. You are love and yet you search for love. It is all right here within you.

Tap your natural resources and let your love pour forth. You are God on high. You are the love and the light. You are all that exists and you are killing you out of fear of not ever finding you. You search in vain for love and it sits right here in you. You search for comfort and you are so powerful you could literally comfort the entire planet. You may give you the greatest gift of all; the gift of unconditional pure love. No strings attached – no ownership, no condemning, just pure sweet love. You may have the greatest relationship of your life simply by tapping into God... you!

Whenever you become light vibration, you become activated to service. You may find that you wish to simply help God, or you may find that you wish to help your family, or you may find that you wish to help everyone. This is how you respond when you are vibrating. You become involved with the whole body of God because you become aware of the whole.

Now; when you begin to serve, you do not need to become a vagabond. It is okay to keep your money and it is okay to keep your belongings. It is also okay to give away your money and it is okay to give away your stuff. It really does not matter. Stuff is simply matter and money is simply the energy you use to create more matter. You may keep it if you like it and you may give it all away if you wish. It is no more important than giving away a rock. You may keep a rock and think it is beautiful, but if you are moving, rocks tend to weigh you down. You may give your rock away or you may simply leave it for someone else to find. A rock is really not own-able, you only think it is.

Now; when you begin to move to your right place you may feel highly motivated to give all your possessions away and no longer "own." This has to do with lightening your load and feeling "free" to flow with no attachments to anyone or anything. This is part of the clearing process and it is not bad or wrong. It is good to let go of all attachments and to know that God will always take good care of you. You cannot lose unless you see life as a loss. You will always win if you see the gift of "freedom from attachments."

Most of you will not wish to go this far at this time. However, those who choose to "let go and let God" in such a strong fashion will see great changes rather quickly. Why? Because you will face your greatest fears. You will dive right into fear of lack and loss. You will see how you do not die from lack and loss. You only die if *you* have decided that it is time; and you will have set up death ahead of time. Most of you will be so involved in learning about your fear regarding loss and lack that you will be very much alive and starvation will never be an issue. You will begin to create situations to challenge your fears and to show you how you have many options when you do not realize that you do. You will open many new doors just by experimenting with your own fears and understanding that the *illusion* of fear is great.

As you move into the future, you will see great changes. Do not fear. You are waking up to the truth and letting go of the lie. Life and death are both the truth and the lie. Life is illusion. Death is illusion. Life does not hurt. Death does not hurt. Money has no value in death, but in life you make it your most valued commodity. It is like shampoo. All matter is meant to move. It circulates. You give away shampoo with no fear of not having more. You do not lock it up in a vault and you do not shoot people to get it. You like it because it helps you, but you do not give it much thought and you don't *fear* not having any. Get this flowing in regards to all matter. Material possessions are here for you to use and enjoy. They were never meant to be fought over and hoarded. All material wealth is simply meant to be used while you are here. Think of earth as a well stocked hotel room and you are the guest. It will do you no good to steal the towels and ashtrays because you are going to die or you are going to ascend, and believe me you will not need them where you are going.

No one will be looking for more money. No one will be looking for more jewelry. No one will be looking for anything material. It simply will not be what is valued. So; if you struggle all your life to *get* more, I suggest you let go of your struggle to get and simply accept what you have as enough, and begin to enjoy being who you are. Look for the good *in* you and look for the good in your life. If it does not feel good change it, and if you do not like being poor work for more, but do it with joy!

*I*t is not difficult to see how you are alone. You have disconnected yourself from yourself. You have gone into total denial of who you are and how you got here. You do not know you because you chose to forget so you could learn anew. You did not choose to forget out of love. You chose to forget out of "desire" to return to this dimension. This dimension was and still is the draw (the attraction). Why do you think you want to stay here and not leave? You are attracted to it and drawn to it just like a moth to a light. The light may zap and kill the moth, but the moth does not care. He believes he must have that light. You believe you must have the material plane. You are addicted.

In the same way that you become addicted to drugs and even obsessed with and addicted to certain people, you are addicted to this dimension of illusion. This is your drug. You do not belong here. You are meant to be God. Come up out of your reverie and become the truth. You are the light, you do not search for the light. You are God; you do not search for God. You must see light in order to be light. You are the love and the light. See the light. Know the light. You are now being drawn to the light, but unlike the moth you will awaken to become the light. You are the light and the love of God. It is that simple.

Now; when you begin to wake up you will be a little uncomfortable. There are many reasons for this. Imagine being on a very powerful hallucinatory drug. When you come off this drug you will be a little off balance until you gain your equilibrium back. Once you are back in balance you will begin to know that you are just experimenting and that God is what you are. You will even know how and why you created all your dreams or circumstances in this dimension. When you wake up you will be happy to know that you are not limited to this third dimension. You will begin to know how you may access all dimensions. Even if you are old (by earth years) you will know that life is just beginning and that you will go on forever and ever. *Everything* is ahead of you. Nothing behind you ever existed and has no meaning.

When you wake up you will feel the love and the light as you will be feeling your own truth. You have shut down your ability to feel in order to exist in the density without pain. It did not work. Now you are going to feel in order to know who you are. You will feel your own divinity. You will feel your own love and you will feel your own godliness. This is the time for coming alive. "The dead will rise up and walk." You are the dead. You think you are alive but you are not. You will learn to become "all that is" and you will know how you are "all that is." It is time now. Come on... wake up.... "See the light!" Be the light. Know the light.

Whenever you feel down, always remember that you are not really here. You only focus your attention so sharply that you *appear* to be here. You are a projection, an apparition. You do not belong here. You are projecting an image. You are a hologram. You are not even here.

So; as you begin to share with others who are not really here, I wish you to remember that they too are holograms. No one is actually here. This is a dream. It is not the truth. It is experimentation. You will begin to see how this all works when you begin to know you better. It is not so much that you are being lied to as you are being tricked by yourself. You are unaware and my job is to make you aware. You are the projection that never returned. Your magnetic field is stuck in this material realm and now it is time to go back to your origins. Don't be afraid to be who you are. Do not be afraid to delve into your own consciousness. Do not be afraid to know your own truth.

You are on a great adventure. You are pulling up stakes and moving. You are going back home to God. God is coming into you to show you who you really are. You will let go of this third dimension of thought and move on to a more productive way of viewing your own creation. This is the dimension of distorted vision. This is the dimension of lies. This is the dimension of reversal. This is the dimension of unreality. When you begin to come *awake* you will begin to see that everything is really the opposite of how it appears. Everything is light but *appears* dark. There is no dark. Darkness is the deception. Only light exists. There is no pain. There is no evil.

Remember how I taught you that your thought literally creates what you see? Well, in this dimension thought is down and must run up. The energy that is running down must change direction and run up. You must *rise* to move out of this dimension. It is the bottom of the barrel and the way out is "up." You must ascend your level of communication and thought. You must rise up to a level of greater clarity of thought. This is salvation. This *is* your way home. The doorway is open and you may rise up and ascend at any time.

The best way to assure your rise is to go within and *adjust* your thinking. Change the way you think and you will rise up out of this dimension. Do not change how you think and you will stay. On the larger scale no one is guilty and no one is innocent, only because there is no guilt, nor is there innocence. It is all a lie. Polarities do not exist. It is one extreme of the exact same energy. You will learn to be innocent by letting go of guilt. You will learn to be guilty by letting go of innocence. It is all the same energy. Guilt is innocence and innocence is guilt. You are lying to yourself if you believe in either polarity. Everything simply is.

Whenever I begin to teach you about love, you begin to know you a little better. Love is not desire and love is not attraction. So what is love? Love is knowing and accepting and allowing. You might even say that love is the *flow* of life. You cannot 'not' love, but you can fear love. The word love is tossed around and the word love is used when it is not meant.

The biggest problem with love seems to be your use of this term. You do not love someone if you have an attraction to them. Attraction is attraction. Love is without attraction. You use love to discuss clothing and dishes and houses and people and jobs and cars. If it feels good you call it love. You do not love a dress that you just have to buy. This is strong desire. You do not love a person you just met. This is strong attraction. You do not love a house without being attached to the dream of living in it. You do not love a child unless you do not care if that child belongs to you or not. Most child love is based on ownership, because you *believe* that you *love* to own. This is not love. This is self-gratification; it is pleasure giving and pleasure getting.

When you truly love, you allow. You *allow* a child to leave you. You allow a lover to leave you. You allow a parent to leave you. There is no desperate holding-on where love is concerned. You have begun to associate love with pain. Love is not pain and pain is not love. Love is to accept and allow and flow. Pain is joy turned around. Joy will lead to pain and pain will lead to joy. If you let go of joy you will have pain and if you let go of pain you will have joy.

So; how did you get so confused about love? You began to use one another and to own one another. You even punish one another in the name of love. It is actually out of anger and resentment that you punish, but you will say it is out of love. You will fight wars out of love of country, and you will kill out of love of your family, or a strong desire to protect them. If you truly love, you will have no problem letting go of everyone and everything. You are not stuck together by love. Love sticks no one to anyone else. You are stuck together out of attraction and you stay together out of need or out of fear of being without he, or she, or your family.

Now; when it comes to family, love is very distorted. Most often you resent and even dislike who you are, so how can you possibly like those who helped to form you into this particular personality? You are so fed up with these people who constantly tell you how to think and eat and live that your resentment for them grows and yet you proclaim to the world that you love them.

Love has lost its way. You no longer know that you are love because you have lost your way. You associate pain with love, and anger with love, and even hatred with love. If you were punished in the name of love as a child, you hate love because love means "you get hit for being bad, because you are loved." *If you wish to hit or strike another, I suggest you do it from truth. You are all confused and creating greater confusion. If you slap or hit a child, be honest enough to say you are doing it out of fear.* Fear is in control on this plane. You strike out at a child or an adult because you are afraid of them, or afraid of losing them. You hit a child if he runs out in traffic because you are afraid he will be hurt or killed, and you could not live with that because your fear of loss is great. You do not hit or strike a child because you love him. This cannot possibly be, since love is a letting go, flowing with, and acceptance of. You are confused!

Now, I suggest you sit down and go within and think about your definition of love and how you got to believe your definition. Each of you have a little bit different twist on what love is and how love should react. I don't think any of you is enlightened where love is concerned. If you were you would not know you, you would know God.

When you become aware, you will no longer feel the need to be fearful. You will find that everything will be love and nothing will be feared. When you become aware, it will not be difficult for you to love, for love is all that you are. You have spent most of your life being afraid and to let go of fear is to let go of most of your life. You are programmed to fear and you are programmed to not trust and you are programmed to not tell the truth.

If you tell the truth you are afraid you will be harmed. You were punished as a child if you confessed to what was considered wrong doing, so now you always lie to protect yourself. You lie in your relationships, and you lie in your work place, and you lie whenever you are afraid of being caught. I want the truth to be told. You must realize that all your lies are digging you in deeper. It is best to be honest and to know that you are not afraid to say the truth. I know that this is a real stretch for you, especially in your relationships. You are all so afraid of losing that you constantly lie to one another. Once you begin to learn that "lying is okay, but the truth will set you free," you will opt for freedom.

Freedom is what this entire situation is all about. No one is meant to be a prisoner of this plane. You are all meant to flow and to move on. It is not necessary to stay locked-in to one way of seeing life, especially if that way is creating greater confusion on this plane.

So; I suggest that you begin to know who you are by telling the truth. Learn to answer from truth and learn to love from truth. You will see soon enough that you do not love at this time, so think how wonderful it will be when you do begin to be love. You will no longer feel the need to lie... ever. You will no longer feel the need to be alone because you will be living your truth and others will not drain you by their presence. Others will no longer have any effect upon your energy field as you will be your honest and truthful self. It is only when you are hiding who you are that you become drained and exhausted by being in the company of those who you believe do not accept you.

Once you learn to love you unconditionally, you will no longer care whether or not anyone accepts you. You will no longer attach to people, and you will no longer *attach* to animals and possessions. Once you begin to love you, you are all that is needed to bring joy and happiness. When you are joy and happiness, you will be more at peace than any amount of money can ever make you. You will find more happiness in your own self than you will ever derive from any relationship. You are the center of your universe, and when you begin to know this truth, you will begin to rise up rapidly to a whole new level or view. You will not be alone by being with you. You will be in the best company ever. You are such a strong, bright light. We must clean off your dust so that you might shine forth to guide the way.

*S*o far you do not wish to be who you are. You are each dependent on your own personality to tell you who you are. If you are a banker you believe you are special and important. If you handle garbage for a living, you believe you are not important. How can this be? Who taught you to believe that a banker is more important than a garbage man? Well, I guess that answers your questions. If you can be taught to respect one above another simply by occupation, you certainly can be taught to respect others above yourself just by identification of wrong or right. You know how wrong you always were as a child. You were told repeatedly the word "No." You know you don't deserve, because you were taught to respect adults and no one ever taught you to respect and admire yourself. As a matter of fact, you were taught to give to others before you give to yourself, and you were taught that to want for yourself is selfish, and we know in this plane that selfish is bad.

So now you are an adult and you have no way of knowing if you are a good person or a bad person. It is all jumbled up *in* you. Part of you tells you how good and lovable you are, but the bigger part says "No, don't you remember, we did this wrong and that wrong? We can't possibly be good or deserve any respect."

You become what you believe you are and what you believe you are is solidified in the cellular memory of your body. We must clean you out. We must drain the information out of you, because it is a lie. You are not bad. You are not wrong. How did you get so messed up? You were taught. And now I am here to "unteach" you. You do not need to fear life nor death. You do not need to punish you for sin. You do not need to beg God's forgiveness for something you never did. What is that something? Sin! There is no sin. Change how you see this and you will be free to enjoy and love you.

You are not evil. You are not bad. You were taught that you are. No! You are not. You are perfect, and only change is going to show you your perfection. Change how you perceive all that occurs and you will begin to rise up out of this mess of lies. This stuff you are stuck to is very, very dense. Let it go. Move up to self-love and self-respect. How can you not *respect* you? You are God.

As long as you continue to be part of this third dimensional reality, you will begin to be third dimensional. When you begin to rise you will know you are leaving this third dimension behind. As long as you stay in matter you are dense. When you rise up out of matter you are light. The only difference between density and light is vibration. Vibration is movement. Stagnation is remaining stuck. As you move, you will see how there is no way you can stay any longer. You will see how you must move in order to grow. It is as simple as growing a plant. If the plant refuses to sprout, and grow limbs, and venture forth, it dies in the dirt. Do not die in the dirt. Rise above this material plane to see above your own contented view.

As you begin to grow in wisdom you will begin to know that you are simply breaking out of an encasement or an egg. You have been in this cocoon or vacuum and now you are simply coming out of it. You are coming alive. You are being born unto God; intelligence; wisdom; knowledge; thought; power; life force. You are not the first and you will not be the last. No one is left out as no one is not *in* God. We all go. We all rise. We all learn. We all grow. We all are God.

When you must leave others behind, you are moving ahead on your path and they are moving ahead on their path. They do not stay put unless they are stagnant in growth and they do not move ahead without assistance. You may have come to assist them and they may have come to assist you. Move on and know that all, absolutely everyone has a place in God. No one is left outside of God. No one is 'not' God. No one is 'not' wisdom. No one is 'not' ignorance. We are all God. We are all part of this plan or we would not be here. The plan is good, the plan is God. The plan is not even aware of itself, however it is in place, it is activated and it is on the rise.

This plan is to explore every dimension, every possibility, every event, every opportunity for growth. This is all done quite simply. You simply learn and grow. You grow by not sticking or holding on and you learn by allowing all to be. See how easy it is to ascend – to rise up out of this mess and destructiveness you live in, in your mind? It is not difficult if you simply see all as good and allow no negative thoughts or judgment regarding self.

Love you my child, for you are this world in all its glory. You created it in your mind and you live *in* it in your mind. You are the fire that started the first spark. You are not, as you believe, the spark that started the fire. You are the fire and you are God. You are the light, and you pretend to be nothing. You are dreaming that you have no importance. You do have importance. Wake up. Know you and you will love you, for it is not possible to not love what is love. Allow you to be, by allowing you to know your own love. Do not beg forgiveness, only beg truth. Do not ask for love but do allow and accept your own love; your own self. You are God on high. You are the most holy of holies. No one is before you and no one is after you. You are the love and you are the light. It is impossible to be more, it is not you to be less.

You will learn that as you grow you may feel growing pains and with pain comes confusion. You will be okay. You were meant to do this. Just as a toddler is meant to grow into an adult, you are meant to be one with God. You my dear sweet child are growing into God.

When we begin to teach only love, we begin to see through the eyes of love. Most of you are so afraid of love that often you see through the eyes of fear. Love is not what you believe. Love does not hurt. Love is not pain. You may love and not get hurt and you may love and not have pain.

If you wish to experience love you may do so without any fear. You simply give out love. You shine your light for all to see. You know you are love and you show what you know. No one is 'not' love, however, everyone does not project love. Love is projected by shining forth what is known as light vibration. If you shine your light on others, you will be allowing you to shine. It is so simple. You get what you give. If you give pain forth you receive pain back, if you give love forth you receive love back. You are conductors of energy and you direct and guide this energy. Often you are not aware of what you do. You do not need to be so strict as to not love. Loving is being who you are. If you love, you do not hug and kiss. Kissing is separate from loving, and hugging is separate from loving. There are no parallels to loving. It is simply being whole in that you *accept* all of you. You embrace all of you and you enjoy all of you.

You do not need to fear love. Love is not "sex." Love is not "hurt." Love is not a state of being attached to another. Those things have to do with relationships and emotions. Love is not so much emotional as it is constant and always and forever! Love does not leave – ever. You do not change love as you change partners. Love stays because love is in you. You are in love. Love is the energy that is you. Love is letting go – letting go of fear and ego and addiction and attachment to. Love is not static. Love moves and grows and changes and accepts and allows for even greater change.

You create your life out of fear and I wish you to come back to love. Love is power and love is peace. Love is not conflict and love is not surrender to outside stimulus. Love is knowing your own self-worth and knowing your own identity and knowing your own God-self. Love allows you mistakes and does not condemn you for walking your path. Love accepts you to the extent that you are. Love protects you, in that you are love and love protects love. You will never find a greater source than love. Love is the blood that runs through the body of God. Love is life force. You cannot give love away. You can however, shine your love forth.

You are so close to discovering your true identity, and once you do, you will be so happy and joyous and love filled. Your future is so bright that you may stand back and be a little timid at first, but this too shall pass. You are the love and the light of this world and you are just now beginning to realize that you are. You may not "feel" this realization yet, but you will. It is right here within your subconscious, and very, very soon you will know who you are. Your subconsciousness will merge so very slowly and gently with your consciousness and we will see quite a change in you then. No one is more pleased about this than me. I am God. I am the light of humanity and I am reaching out to you to feed your consciousness. This is indeed a very great time of awakening – when God can speak to his children and they will listen without fear, without criticism and without judgment. God is indeed *growing* in love, and judgment is falling away. You are the love and the light of the world. Share what you are and love all.

When you begin to know how you came here to become God, you will no longer wish to punish. You will not wish to punish you and you will not wish to punish others. It is not so much that you consciously do this, but more that you have a habit of punishment. Punishment began long ago and was especially admired in some religions and certain cultures.

Hanging on the cross was only one form of punishment. You also had your floggings and even torture chambers. Everyone knew that you were liable to be punished for your errors and so you began to do good just to avoid punishment. You still teach punishment. You still believe in a punishing God who puts you in hell if you're bad. Your entire culture is based on good and bad, or good and evil. I wish you to let go of evil and see only good. Let go of punishment and the idea that everyone must pay somehow for their mistakes.

It is not enough that you create pain, but now you create confusion regarding pain. How? Well, sometimes you punish those who are guilty of nothing, and you apologize to them after you have severely beaten or imprisoned them by mistake, and this creates great confusion around right and wrong because now (by your rules) you become the wrong doer. It is not right nor is it wrong. It is simply not necessary. You will learn at some point that all creation takes care of its own. You do not *allow* this at this time but you will learn.

You will also learn to be happy with you and to let you go without punishment. You will no longer flog yourself which is what you do when you create disease within your body. You create all of this to punish you for your wrong, or your bad ways. It is not necessary. No one need ever be sick, or tired, or old. It is simply not necessary.

You began to believe that you could not convince your body to heal, and you began to believe that you were not good enough to heal. You began to show signs of not wanting to heal by letting disease take over. You gave way for disease by not loving you. You began to attach to a belief system that says that you are not good, and this belief is what is killing you. You are God and you do not need to be punished by disease, or accidents, or imprisonment. You are holy.

When you begin to vibrate at the speed of light you will no longer find pain or anything else in your energy field. You will be pure. You will see through the eyes of purity and you will not be afraid. No fear will be in your aura as you will have transformed love to light. You will have lifted up your burdens and given them over to God. You do not need to be so afraid of turning your life over to God. It is not such a bad deal once you get the hang of it.

You will find that as you go along your path you will have less fear and more doubt and uncertainty. This uncertainty comes from fear, however fear fades as you move closer to the truth. So, you will still have your doubt and your uncertainties, however you will have much less fear which means you will have a great deal more courage. With courage you may look at your fears and gain insight into you. You may find that you do not belong so much to your fears as you thought and you may discover how easily you can outgrow fear.

So; as you move along, you begin to drop off parts of you that are no longer needed, and these parts will be replaced by new enlightened parts who are not afraid and who know God to be self-evident. These new parts will begin to guide you even as you are being doubtful and insecure. These new parts are new sparks of intelligence within you. They are now working to guide you into your proper place for ascension so that you may rise above this current level of seeing all. When you begin to feel these new parts you may also feel the old you tugging away at your mind. This is to be expected. Old habits and old patterns die hard. You are witnessing the death of an old way of viewing life and the birth of the new. This death is known as the end of this world as it is now known.

No big calamity must take place for your world to

end. Only you must change. No one else must change and the earth need not explode or slip off into the ocean. A very simple thing will occur. Life will change for you, because your view finder has been cleaned up. It's that simple. No big explosion no big turmoil, no huge fight to survive the ravages of an ending world. This may take place inside of you, but you will do well with this change.

For those of you who await the darkness and gloom of outer destruction, I suggest you give it up. What you believe is what you get to keep. Hold tight to your belief in destruction and you will be *allowed* to see destruction. In holding on to it you are requesting it. It is so easy to let go of it. You simply say, "Not in my world. This will not occur in my world, as my world is full of peace and love and truth." Only in a world of pain would you see great destruction, and you my dear sweet child are moving out of pain. You will no longer *need* to bring hurt to anyone for any reason. Belief in destruction is based in a belief or need for punishment. *Let it go.* There is no need for pain on this planet or on any other. No big traumas here, only love and peace and joy and happiness. Believe in these and let go of all the rest.

You are now in a position to know love. You will find that when you begin to look at all parts of you; you will begin to accept all parts of you. It is in the knowing that you learn to accept. If no one ever told you how to accept and love yourself, you would have no way of knowing. Only in learning can you know and only by memory can you learn. Memory is what you are made of and all memory is written in you. You are literally a product of your memory. What you have been taught to *believe* regarding life is what you believe regarding you. You are not so much a product of your imagination as you are a product of fear and mistrust and lack of faith in God.

As you begin to learn and to grow, you will begin to discover faith in God and you will once again trust in God. You are not so afraid of God as you once were and this is good. To put the fear of God in you is to fear your own self. I do not wish this type of fear tactic to be used regarding yourselves. You are love and light, you are not some monster who wishes to punish everyone for everything.

I am teaching you how to love you out of love. It is not so difficult as you believe. As you learn, you take off the layers of past programming and past beliefs that amount to nothing more than superstition. You are so afraid to be God that you have buried your true identity, and of course why would you wish to admit who you are? You have been taught of a God who sits in judgment and condemns people to hell, and floods this planet out of unrestrained anger. He is an ogre – this God you believe to be so mighty. You say you love him, but in actuality you fear him. You are afraid he will kill you or send you to hell. I want you to know that when you worship a God who you are afraid of, you are worshipping fear. Fear is not love. Fear is the love energy running backward. Love is "absence of fear" and fear is "absence of love."

You may bow to him and pray to him and ask him to forgive you so he won't punish you, but you are worshipping the false God. God is love. God does not possess fear. God is the opposite of fear. God is faith and love. Nothing else is God. No one else is God. You have created a false *image* of God, and this image is just as false as the golden calf image. It is a lie. God is truth. God is love. God does not judge and God is you.

You are not only the most powerful being to arrive on this plane, you are also the biggest. You are everlasting, on-going, infinite beingness. No one else is you and you are no one else. You are all "one" and you are separate only by personality. Your memory creates your personality and your thoughts, beliefs and emotions create your memory. Most of you are made up of a wide variety of memory, which was formed by your belief in good or bad. Evil plays a big role in memory, and hopefully you will begin to see how God is you and evil is not.

No one is ever meant to be evil. It is not possible for you to be evil, as your true identity is love and light. Once you begin to see how you are love and light you will no longer judge yourself as less than your true identity. As you begin to grow and take on layer after layer of truth, your entire personality may look different. You may respond differently and you may look at life differently. As you take on these new layers of belief, you are building a solid foundation to grow on. You are stripping off the old and building the new, one step at a time. You are beginning to see how to create a whole new you, without the old habit, or pattern, of sloughing off the body and going out to return and try again in a new body. This time you are going to transform, without death and reentry, or reincarnation.

You are going to begin a new pattern that will become very popular. This pattern we will call transformed ascension. Yes; this is a very good name for what we are doing here. So; all of you are being transformed to ready you for ascension. You can tell when you begin to transform, by the way you begin to lose the old way of holding on to life and people and places and things. Life is meant to flow and love is meant to flow. No attachments please. Do not be attached to people or things or thoughts or beliefs or life. Let it all go. None of it is important if you wish to rise above it all and move to the higher dimension of love.

To stay stuck in matter is to stay attached to this third dimensional illusion, as you now know it. To let go of it and rise up you simply "let it go." You rise above a set belief in "hanging-on at all costs." Let go of everything. Float free. Know the joy of floating in God. Do not hold on to old truths and superstitions and fears. Throw up your hands and surrender to God. God is you. Let God do what God does. God is love and you are screaming for love. You are restricting God by not allowing him to do what he does, or is. He is life itself. He is light. He is infinite. He is almighty powerful wisdom. Get it together and let God reign in you. Let God step forward. Get him up and out of his hiding place. Make him king, or her queen for a day.

Once you begin to communicate with God you will know that God really exists in you. You will begin to see how you are part of God. This will lead to the discovery that you are connected to God and God is connected to you. This will allow you to let go of your hold on life, as you now see it. You will begin to see so many possibilities just by letting you be God. It is that simple. Let you be God. Give yourself the gift of God. Allow you to be good enough to be God, to be love, to be light. You are, you know? You are so much, and your mind is so small that you see yourself as so small. Open up. Let God in. Let God take over and you will be letting love in and allowing love to take over.

The choice as always is yours. The gift as always is for you, and the love as always is right here where it has always been. Release love. Set love free to conquer fear. Let go of your fears and walk in trust and faith without fear. You think you might get hurt or killed if you walk in trust and faith, but even pain and death are not what you have made them out to be. Death may be a most enjoyable experience and you may wish to experience death to let go of your fear of death.

What I am teaching you in this class is that you are

never alone. You are never without God and there is no bad thing that can ever happen to you. Even if you die, you will go back to God. How can that be bad? Do not fear anything. Know that for a child of God all experience holds a gift. This is part of what Jesus knew and this is how he walked with courage to his hanging. He did not see it as bad. He saw it only as his return to God. It's really that simple. No one can control you and no one can have power over you if you know the simple truth. The simple truth is that all life is good. Everything contains a big gift and you, my child of God, need only tune in to see the good. If you look for the good you will always find it. It is there. You have spent many lifetimes searching for judgment, which creates bad and evil. Give up this search and begin to look only for the good in all things.

When we begin to realize how beat up and down trodden we are, we will want to change and begin to love instead of hate our own individual personality. We have come to a point of understanding where we know that it is not necessary to beat up and submit to self-abuse. It is not necessary to hurt you – not ever. It is not necessary to punish you – not ever, and it is not necessary to be in fear of being punished – not ever. You will find that as you begin to clear and rise, you will begin to see in a whole new light. You will no longer see the past as offensive and you will no longer see yourself as offensive.

As you begin to grow in light you will begin to see the good in all and you will know that you are not alone. You will see how all are connected and how one affects the other. You will see how in healing yourself you start a chain reaction that reaches out to touch others. It is not that you ignite them so much as you inspire them on a subconscious level. Some will begin to change and not even notice, others will try very hard to change and not get far. It is all a matter of timing and learning to unlayer or take off what you know in order to take in the truth.

As you learn to raise your own vibration you will learn to see from a new perspective. As you do this, you will become free of all the old programming and childhood grievances that you hold. You will be transformed by the light. You will become a light being. You will literally vibrate at the speed and velocity of energy. You will be a spark flying through time and space with no attachment to time and space. You will move freely through anything, as you will no longer be attached to matter through your fear of losing matter. You will move at will through time and space. You will have the ability to project your thought body forward in time, or backward in time. You will come to the realization that you *are* all time and space.

You are the Second Coming of God. You are God collecting and *recollect*-ing his thoughts. He projected you out, now he is reeling you back in. He is now remembering what he forgot. He thought and it was made to move. He thought again, and again it was moved. He thought for a very long time, and as his train of thought moved from one place of creation to the next, he literally left it there to go on to his next thought. Now he is retracing his steps in order to find lost thought. You are the thought that is now being recollected. Do you remember? He thought you up. He began by remembering how he wanted to view his own beingness. He sent out thought after thought on this subject and now he is remembering in what order the thoughts were projected so he might retrieve them as they went out.

He is spinning a big ball of yarn full of old thought that has been discarded. He is rewinding his idea in order to create a new idea. He will not wish to wait long, as his new idea is already projecting forth and it is only a matter of time before new idea takes precedence over old thought that is lost in chaos.

As God retrieves all parts of himself, he is creating quite a stir and it will be felt. It will not be painful for those who wish to return, and therefore show no resistance. Those who flow forward toward him need not *feel* pulled at. Those who *hold on* may feel pulled at. This is a time of great change. This is a very big awakening, and most of you who have read this series from God are being taught to *let go and flow, so you will not feel pain.* As you learn the techniques I have taught, you will learn how holding on creates resistance, and going with the flow creates movement forward. You cannot move forward without the help of light. Light is movement, in that it vibrates and spins and is not dense nor is it stagnant.

You have done well in this class. You are learning

and growing and spinning and growing and spinning and moving. You will return to love. You will see all clearly and you will learn how to love you once again. It is not long now. You will know ascension when you feel the movement in you. You will know you are rising when you just can't seem to get angry or upset even when you think you should. On the day that someone hits you or insults you and you just don't feel the *urge* to retaliate or get upset, you are beginning to let go of pain and hurt and feel only love. It will happen right after you let go of your belief in pain and hurt.

You will begin to see only the good in all things and you will begin to know only love, and nothing else will have power over you. You will let go of all the old ways of acting and reacting and you will be "free" for the first time in a very, very long time.

When you begin to vibrate you begin to speed things up. Most of you do not wish to stay stagnant and so you are now creating movement. If you see great change and movement in your life it's simply because you have decided to stop remaining stagnant.

As you go along, you will see how you do not always know how to be changeable. The best way I know of, to be changeable, is to flow. Do not resist change.

Allow all change to occur and be flexible enough to move *with* the change. As you learn to move with change, you will also be learning how to change. The only difference between stagnation and change is disease. Disease grows and breeds in stagnation. Life grows and breeds in change.

When you get to the point that you no longer care how you are being changed and you know that you are growing from this change, you will no longer fear others, or what they say, think or do. You will be totally "free" to accept yourself without judgment against yourself. Most of you are still judging you at every turn. When you see others judge you, it is to show you how you judge you. When you no longer judge you, you will not hear others judge you.

You are growing into a being of light and a being of light is not concerned with the thoughts of others. A being of light knows who he is and knows he is love. When you are love you simply shine love, regardless of what is occurring around you. You will know that you are the projector and the world around you is the visually projected image. As *you* heal, this image will heal; as you take on light, this image will take on light, and as you move to a new level, or view, so might your projected image. Do not be upset when people or things leave you. You are moving *up* to a new viewpoint and people who belong to the old view will remain in the old view.

As you raise your level of consciousness, you will literally begin to spin like a top. You will vibrate, and spin with this vibration. You will then project new images and they will move and change as you move and change. Most of what you are doing at this time has to do with getting unstuck from your stagnation. As you get more and more unstuck, you will be freer and freer to be light vibration. Once you have achieved light vibration, you will know you are your creator. It is not possible for you to reach this level without knowledge of your true identity.

You are now on this path to life-giving freedom and you are now on your way home. You will not know how you are until you are well. Confusion is great at this time and to get you moving creates greater confusion. You might say "we are stirring things up," and in the stirring "the shit may fly." After all, it is a big decayed mess we are dealing with and this mess is right inside of you and most of it can be cleaned out of you, by cleaning out your bowels. Don't let decay and disease take over. Use your enema to keep you cleaned out and smooth running. This is no joke. Enema works. It is not only life saving, it is spiritually balanced. It allows your body to right its own imbalance, by removing positive and negative charges of energy that are locked in the electrolytes you are removing. You may not understand this, but you will get great relief from it.

It is not so difficult to teach you something you do not already know, but it is most difficult to teach you something that you do not wish to accept because (you think) you know better. I will allow you your own choice on the enema issue. I am here only to teach and to show you how, on a simple human level, you too may achieve advanced reparation from all the damage that has already been done. This is not a forced issue. This is simply an example of how you wish to stay where you are, rather than *accept* a small, new idea. So; how flexible are you?

So far you have not been put upon to do anything that is out of line for your character. Most of you are in a good state of mind and you are ready to change. When you begin to see how change will affect you, you will not be so anxious for it, but you will accept it. It is for your own good. This good is a much higher good than neediness. This good is a much more fulfilling good than self-gratification. This good is an all encompassing good that affects your entire well-being. It is for your body and your mind as well as your spirit.

When you begin to raise your vibration, you are going to see how what you once thought to be very important is now not so important. Freedom comes in many forms. You have taught yourself to be free by buying your way to freedom. You feel that if you only have enough money you will not have to depend on others, nor will you have to answer to others. In actuality, the opposite is true. High finance traps you in a giant circle of answering to everyone and being available, or your house or empire will crumble. The freedom is now lost in a maze of contracts and follow-throughs. When you begin to rely on money for freedom, you are actually returning freedom for prosperity. You are giving up to the power of the dollar and it is ruling your life.

Now; do not get me wrong here. I am not saying give your riches away. I am saying do not be a slave to your empire. That is no more freedom than being trapped in poverty. Who has more free time, a man with an empire to run or a man with a nine to five job and weekends free? You may be trading in your freedom because you actually think you are creating greater freedom and flexibility. In actuality you are trading in your time for money, in hopes that the money will set you free. When you desire freedom, I highly suggest you ask for freedom and not money. Many of you are very confused in this area. You ask for prosperity and money when what you really want is joy and peace of mind. If joy and peace of mind are your goal why don't you ask for joy and peace of mind?

As you begin to see how happy you can be, you will wish to *allow* whatever happens to bring joy and peace of mind your way. You will not be locked in to prosperity. What if joy and peace of mind were given to you through someone who granted you freedom, and access to everything your heart desires? Would it be fair to suggest that this was a gift and you do not own this gift, however you are being given free reign to enjoy this gift? This is how all creation works. You are to be allowed to use and enjoy and partake, but not own. You may access many gifts yet never own a single one.

This is flowing and this is how creation is meant to be, free and yet a big gift; no ownership, only care-taking; receiving and giving – receiving and giving. As you begin to see how this works you will begin to know that you too are prosperous, and you too may create great gifts out of thin air. It does not take much to be free and it does not take much to have peace of mind. To be free, simply put down your burden and unlock your shackles which tie you to people and property. To have peace of mind, simply unload your fears and allow love to take over.

I know this is all a big stretch for you, but this is a time for stretching and growing. Do not be so afraid to be free. Do not be so afraid to let go of everything. You will not fall. You are *in* God and there is no bottom to hit. You are simply suspended in God and growing in mid air. Your fears of falling are invalid and you will soon see how this works. You are safe my child. You have never been in danger. As a matter of fact, there is no danger.

Well into this bright new way of viewing your life, you will discover that you have actually left your old self behind. You will see how you drop off old belief systems and take on new thought. As you move through time and space, you begin to recollect yourself by remembering who and what you are.

As certain parts of you begin to remember, they also begin to ascend. As they ascend, they transform to light until you are simply one giant light beam. This is your true identity. You are a beam of light. You do not shine now because you are not cleaned out and cleaned up. Once you get cleaned out you will feel better. This cleaning out process is different for each individual and will take as much time as required by the unconscious, unknown parts of self. As you begin to clean you out, you will see how you do not need to hold on to old ways in order to survive. You will begin to see how you do not love "self" and even how you hate "self." You will begin to know that you are in a state of transformation simply by realizing how badly you need fixing. Realizing you need fixing is sometimes the first step. Most often you will insist that all the others need fixing in order to meet your needs

As your needs grow less and less, you may actually become more needy and push to get your remaining needs met. This is sort of like giving up and yet wanting more. When you feel like you want more, you usually start pushing at someone to get those needs met. This may create some friction and this too can be useful, in that you may release pent up frustration and pain as you search to fulfill your needs. As you search for ways to fulfill your needs, you begin to see how desperate you are to have these needs met. Once you know how much desperation you carry, you will be able to recognize your fears. Fear leads to desperation and desperation is strong desire turned into anger at not having one's needs met.

Now; most needs are very basic. There is need for food, need for shelter and need (this one is actually desire) for a mate. The need for food is well understood and you all sympathize with those who do not have food. The second basic need is for shelter and this need is often tied in with cooperation and needy receptive handling. This means simply that in order to receive shelter you must handle your landlord with kid gloves or you are out on your ear. So, basically this need is met by cooperative giving to insure your own private space. The last basic need is for a mate and this need is not exactly life threatening. You do not die or get rained on if you don't have a boyfriend or a girlfriend. This need or desire has been created out of fear of loneliness, and it is out of fear of never loving or being loved that you search for your mate. Low self-esteem drives you in this search.

Now; to get your basic needs met you will push and lie and cheat and steal. This is how needy you are and this is how strong your fear of loss is in these three areas. You have created a situation for yourself that is quite unusual. You are a light beam and now you have transformed to the extent that you do not know how to be you any longer. You do not know that you will always provide for all your basic needs and more. You do not remember that being a light is being electric and being electric has charge and *creates.*

So now you wallow in your self-pity, and I want you to start concentrating on creating less material need and greater spiritual need. Meet your spiritual needs first. Feed you love, lots and lots of self-love. Do not give all of your good intentions and generosity to everyone but you. Put you first, not last. As you well know, when you put spirit last you get to stay with you and spirit must wait his turn. You will see how this works soon. No one is in you but you. And if you do not acknowledge spirit, what have you got? Just you. You – being all that programming that says you're bad, you're guilty, you're a sinner. Leave you behind and come aboard spirit. Ride spirit home to truth. Leave all the garbage and programming for another, if that is how they choose to experience this plane. There are many ways to experience this plane, and only one of them is to get down in it and become part of it. Let go of that way. That is kindergarten class. You are in the tenth grade. Come up to this level of thinking. Rise above the material plane with its basic fears and basic needs.

You too can go into a desert for forty days and forty nights and survive. It is all a level of programming, and eventually you will wish to rise to this new level. Food needs are not true needs. Spiritual food will guide you to rise above material food. You did not always eat. It was not always a necessity, and we can reverse spin and develop to the same level of trust that is needed to provide a process that does not require food.

You are fooling yourself if you think that you are not capable of meeting all your own needs at any time of the day or night. You will create out of thin air when you begin to remember who and what you are. None of this that you find in the illusion of this third dimension is real, nor is it true. Transcend it and grow to want more light.

Whenever I talk to you about love, you do not know what I am talking about. Love is self-acceptance and knowledge that you are God. Until you reach this state of self-acceptance you will be alone in your fear. Most of what you teach regarding love is actually "kindness to others." You teach one another to be kind and gentle with those you care about, but you forget to teach others to be kind and gentle with themselves. This is not bad; it is just creating off-balance. You project images of yourself and you are taught to be kind to your images but what about you? What about the projector itself? How can you project lovable images if the projector itself is not lovable?

You will learn to love the self by letting you be. Everything I taught you about not beating-up-on or pushing at others, I want you to bring back to the self. Do not beat up on you. Do not push at you. Leave you alone. Let you be. Accept you as you are. This may sound contradictory to what I have been teaching you about change, but it is not. It is enough to want change. It is not necessary to judge and abuse yourself for not changing quickly enough.

Change is always instantaneous in that the moment you decide to change, change begins to occur. You may not see the effects of change overnight, but in the "desire for" you receive. It is not necessary for you to sit and watch every word you say and every move you make. This creates greater fear of losing.

So; begin to love you by allowing you to be who and what you are at every moment of every day. Love you by allowing you to be, and by accepting that you are God in a state of becoming God.

⁂

You are not to be so full of guilt about living. You are meant to be only love; joy, peace, happiness and light. Somehow you got it all so confused that you began to fear. You fear being joyful and you fear peace. You are afraid that if you get too much joy it will end. You are afraid that if you have too much peace you will get bored. You constantly create more and more friction just to keep you moving in opposing directions.

You are not so much out of balance as you are out of you. No one is running you. You are part of this big creation and yet you have deserted you. You no longer wish to be you. You no longer *care* for you. You are looking to be cared for by others. You must learn now to *care* for your own self.

As a child you come into this world and you are told how you are loved and cared for by others. You learned about care from those who taught you that you were in their care and keeping until you could care for yourself. They did not always take good care of you because, like you, they did not know how to care about and for themselves. So, how can they possibly teach you to care for and love yourself?

Now is the time! This is a time of great awakening and this is a time to learn how to love and care for you. You constantly hand yourself over to others in hopes that they will care for you. You put them on a pedestal, and look up to them, and offer them your kindness and affection in order to bribe them into *caring* for you. You do not love you, so how can you possibly care for you? You care for others and even take responsibility for their actions. You do not, however, care for you. You only know how to be in someone else's care and this is why you are searching for your mate. Your twin soul is not you. You are you and your twin soul is your other half. You must love you enough to care for you.

Now; I wish you to spend today taking real good care of yourself. This is how you will do this. You will acknowledge you as a very special guest who is most lovable and enjoyable to be with. Then you will share your time and your day with you. Be conscious of you. Know that you are in this body as well as out of it. Begin to talk to you. Why do you never talk to you? Why do you ignore you? How can you ignore God? You are so confused, that is how. But, the good news is, that God is here and you are on the rise.

Okay now, I want you to begin by talking to you and showing you around, and taking real good care of you for this day. You are a royal visitor and you deserve royal treatment.

When I ask you to be love, I do not expect you to go around and give your belongings and your money to everyone you wish to help. That is assisting others and has little to do with love. Love is not giving gifts and love is not hugging and kissing. Love is mutual consent and agreement to accept you as you are. Love is letting you be by allowing yourself to be without judgment against you for past sins.

You are not meant to be judged for every little (or big) thing that you do. Judgment is the key to unlock the doors to love. Let go of judgment and all else will fall into its proper place. You are not meant to be in judgment, you are meant to be in love. As you begin to grow in love, you will begin to leave judgment behind. You will know when you have stopped judging yourself, as you will no longer see you judging others.

You see, you are a non-prejudicial judger. You judge all as you judge yourself. You will easily see how much judgment you have let go of by looking at how harshly you condemn others. If you have strong dislike of others, then you can be sure that you have strong dislike of yourself. If you hate someone for their intolerance, then you can be sure that you hate you for your own intolerant behavior. If you do not believe in the love and light of another, then you can rest assured that you do not believe in your own love and light. If you believe someone is possessed by evil, it is only a reflection, that you believe you too carry evil.

Nothing is ever shown to you that is not in you. You have learned to disguise yourself and to point the finger of blame, when you are actually pointing at your own projected image. So; how do you deal with and tolerate your own images? You will learn to let them go. They do not mean much, and are only here to assist you in seeing who and what you are. Learn to accept them and learn that they are not yours to own, nor are they yours to take responsibility for. They are simply a direction finder, a finger pointing and saying, "Look, this may be what you are doing to you!"

Do not be so afraid of your reflections that you traumatize yourself. I know you deal with violence and brutality, but I wish you to rise above such nonsense. I wish you to love and accept your own good to the extent that you get out of the way when someone (a reflection of your inner turmoil) decides to unload on you or release his or her anger on you. My pen has explained it this way to a friend. She simply sees all anger as toxic illness and when someone explodes with violence or anger, they are vomiting their toxic waste. Liane decided long ago not to be the target of anyone's anger. She simply leaves. She decided that anger releasing is often like vomiting up illness and when someone vomits she gets out of the way. She doesn't care to get any of it on her. It is no different with anger and abuse. Do not get involved. Leave!

When you begin to raise your level of thinking, you begin to see more clearly. You have far less confusion and a much greater sense of being at one with yourself. Most importantly, you begin to know that you are not bad. You begin to realize that you are becoming God through a process of allowing God in. It is just that simple. Allow God into you and you become God. Deny God and you block his entrance. God is you, so in denying God, you are in effect denying you. There is no simpler way to put it. You are God and God is you. You do not change this; you simply allow it or not allow it, accept it or not accept it.

You will find that to accept God is to accept love, and light, and peace, and joy, and happiness. This is simply because you will be accepting what you already are. You are now in a state of change, and change is what will teach you to rise above all complaisance to a level of self-love and respect and honor. You are not so afraid of being God as you are afraid of waking up to the fact that you are not who you currently believe you are.

When you believe you are not God, you believe a lie regarding who you are. In believing this lie you create mistrust within your own consciousness. Mistrust in you creates mistrust in life and often is followed by stress, resentment and eventually anger, hatred, and harm to the self. This harm may appear in the form of an accident or an illness, but it is still harm to the self, by the self.

You will learn at some point that you do not know how to love you because you will not accept the fact that you are God. You are the creator of all life and you have moved into your creation to see how it feels. Now it is time to wake up and know that it is all you and it is all okay, and good, and right. No wrong here, only good is here, only right is here, only love is here, and only God is present.

When you begin to know that you are God, you will see that you do no wrong. You may make choice after choice without judgment against any choice. You may choose to be an artist or a rapist and it will simply be a choice. You will not be hung up on right and wrong. You will not judge you for wrong, for you will know that a choice is nothing more than an expression of emotion, and emotion is nothing more than release of pain.

Pain is often misunderstood. It is an emotional trigger for your explosive behavior. Pain is the bullet in your gun and pain is also the trigger that ejects the bullet. If you had no pain in you, you would never have an upsetting day or event or thought. All upset comes from pain. Pain is emotional as well as physical. Pain may be experienced or denied. If you choose denial, you will still get to see your pain at some point. If you choose to forget your pain, it is still in you. The only way to let go of your pain is to release it, in a healthy way, onto your emotions. Pain, as an emotion, will show you a great deal about yourself.

When you release your pain, you may begin to have a great deal of judgment against others. This is simply a sign that judgment is now moving in you in order to release more pain. You see, judgment and pain work together. It is association. When I used the word rapist, you were uncomfortable because you associate rape with pain. When I said artist you relaxed because there is no pain association with art, not for most of you anyway.

So, this is how you work inside. This is what makes you tick. Everything is connected to pain or to joy. If something is connected to pain, you judge it as bad so you will not *experience* the pain you associate with it. You are not wrong to judge. This is simply a technique that you developed since you lost your ability to perceive knowledge and wisdom. You once perceived everything from a much larger view point without your current limitations. This perception allowed you the freedom of greater experiential choices, as you were not afraid of pain. Now you fear pain and you fear love as painful, so it is very difficult to convince you to love you no matter how awful you *think* you might be.

Be afraid of nothing and allow everything to be experienced. Do not judge what has or has not occurred in your life and you will no longer hold on to pain. You will know that you were hurt, yes, but it is not terminal. You will learn that you do not have to live in the pain. You may come forward and express your pain and allow it to release. You are not the cause of your pain and you are not even the effect. You are simply love, and you got confused as to what you are and you began to hold on to something that was simply an experience associated with pain. Do not own it. Do not become it.

Look at your pain and by all means express it. Do not harm you and do not harm others, but *do* express it. Say the words and get it up and out. Get it moving in you so it can come up out of you. Say, "I have pain. I hurt." Then begin to ask to be shown where this pain was denied and where this pain began. You will release pain by accepting that you hold pain. You will not release pain by convincing your mind that it does not exist. Live in acceptance and allow everything to be accepted for what it is. Do not take on greater pain by continuing to judge. Judgment creates such a great hold on pain. Let go – let God!

You are not the only one who is in pain. You each have your own beliefs and you each hide from your own fears. As you learn to explore and invade your own fears and pain, you will discover how easily you slip from pain to joy and from darkness to light. You will discover that you are no longer dense with pain and fear. You will discover that you are light and you are good. As you begin to see how you are light, you will begin to know your own truth.

You spend a great deal of time with you and yet you do not truly know you. You only think you do.

As you begin to move ahead, you will begin to discover how you came to be who you are. Who you are is a conglomerate of all that you have experienced and taken on. Most experience is not you. You felt it so now you own it, but you may release it at any given moment. In the releasing comes the joy of knowing it is not real. You experience, so you buy. Do not buy. You may experience without "buying into" if you can let go of judgment. Judgment keeps you stuck to, and judgment keeps you *in* a particular situation. Without judgment there is no pain and without judgment there is no past to invade your present.

Judgment causes all parts of you to stay in the past experience that you are so busily judging. When you are so *involved* with a situation, you spend all of your time figuring out how to deal with it. It is now projected into your present and begins to take over. The more energy that is used to negotiate with this experience, the greater impact it has on your present.

So; if you project thought into the past, you bring the past into focus in the present moment. You do not project back to the incident in the past. You literally bring the past up to you in the present moment. Therefore, you are moving time. Therefore, you are moving space. You are all time and all space. You are God and you project in and out of you at will. You are not only all time and space, you are life and death. You are infinity. You *are* the past, the present and the future. You are all in one. You are the one in all.

You will learn to discover who you are by learning to know you. Look at you. Look into you. You are God. Spend some time with you. Stop running from you and begin to love you. Every time you run from you, you create greater separation between who you are and what you believe you are. Let you integrate by allowing you to be good, by allowing you to be desirable, by allowing you to be God.

Whenever you show yourself love, you are showing yourself your true colors, for love is what you are, and love is all you can ever really be. Allow you to be the best by allowing you to accept yourself without judgment against any part of you. You are God, you are love, you are light. Know it, accept it and allow it.

When you begin to know you, you will have crossed over into self-discovery. You will have seen the beginning and the end of your creation. You may begin with your death and work back to your birth or you may begin at birth and work forward to your death. Do not be afraid to look at birth and do not be afraid to look at death.

Today is December twenty-fifth and most of you celebrate this day as a day of birth. Do not forget to celebrate death. Death is simply the completion of this birth cycle and it is in death that you feel peace and calm and serenity. So, if you yearn for peace and tranquility, why do you suppose that you fear death, which is actually peace to most?

Suppose you were to go through your own death prematurely, and see and feel everything that you would see and feel in the actual experience. Would you then wish for death to come sooner? Can death be as great and beautiful as birth? Maybe we should celebrate death and throw a party every year on the anniversary of a loved one's death. You do not celebrate death because you fear death. Stop fearing that which you do not understand. If you understood death, you would never mourn and you would never punish by death. You are so silly to punish by death. You actually give the unpardonable one *total freedom* by putting him to death. This is indeed a very big gift.

So; how did you get so confused and begin to worship life and fear death? You are superstitious, that is how. You think that when someone is out of view they are gone, and so you freak out and cry and scream out of fear of loss. It is like a baby when you leave their sight – "Oh no, my mommy and daddy have left me. What will I do now?" I guess crying seemed the best answer to you, and that's how you've handled death for centuries. Now I wish you to change. I wish you to rejoice at death, and to laugh and dance and know that freedom from body feels very good to those who have left their body. So; how can you be so cruel as to laugh and dance at grandpa's funeral? Well, until this process is accepted, I highly suggest you celebrate in private. But do celebrate. It will help not only you, it will also help the one who is leaving. You see, everything is connected to everything else.

I wish you a Merry Christmas and an especially enlightened New Year!

So far you are not afraid to love as long as you feel free to escape. You do not wish to love and be stuck in it. You feel like love is a commitment, when in actuality love is simply love. Love has no strings attached and love does not mean doing everything for the one you love. That is taking over and taking responsibility for. It is not love. To love is to know and accept. Not to own and keep, but simply to know and accept.

To accept is to realize one another's faults and to realize you are learning and growing and to accept that fact. Accepting does not mean staying with anyone or even having a relationship with them. You may choose your relationships in the same way that you choose a car. If you like the way it runs and looks, go for it. A relationship is an adventure with another person and has little to do with love. Love is much bigger and has no limits.

You do not love just one mate; that is a *rule* that you have created to keep you safe from losing. You do not lose people because you do not own people. You however, have a very difficult time when I suggest you don't own. Floating free seems to frighten you. You believe that to have freedom is to have chaos. This assumption is incorrect. Freedom without limitation creates expansion without limitation. Control and limitation creates implosion and great stress. You are imploding *in* on yourselves because you have created a rule that says you are limited beings. You are not limited, you are limitless. You are choking you to death with your rules and your punishments, that you so freely use to stop you or keep you safe.

Let go of all these rules and allow truth and freedom to come forward. You have been lying to yourselves for such a long time that it would be quite refreshing if you began to speak the truth without fear of a mob scene. Most of you are so afraid of what the others will think that you spend all of your energy pleasing them. Stop pleasing others. Please you by accepting you, and if you are meant to be accepted by others you will be.

So far you have not been too upset by your fears. You have been very gentle in dealing with yourself and you have not questioned your own approach. This, however, is not your only choice. You may become more familiar with your fear by experiencing fear. If you fear heights you might climb to the top of a mountain or take an elevator to the top of a tall building. You will begin to activate your fear by going into your fear. If you fear rain, you might walk in the rain and if you fear fire, you might experiment with fire to see what frightens you about it. This is called facing your fears head on. If you do not wish to face your fears, you might never know you fully. Only in facing what you fear will you combine enough fear energy to support the belief in the fear completely. As the energy builds around this fear you get to see more and more how you created this fear.

If you fear groups of people, put yourself in groups and see why you fear this situation. If you fear being alone, I suggest you go somewhere to be alone for awhile. This will allow you to experience what you fear and maybe learn that it is not so bad after all. Something taught you to believe in good or bad situations, so now you spend your time avoiding what you feel are bad situations. What I would like you to do is to learn that not only does bad not exist, it is all simply experience. If you can learn to stay or leave at will, you will no longer fear certain situations with certain people.

You feel trapped in certain situations only because you are afraid to be yourself. If you are uncomfortable around a specific person I suggest you leave. Do not make yourself stay and be put down or put upon. You may always leave. Don't begin to fear facing certain people, or dealing with certain people who seem to upset you. Go into each situation knowing that you will respond in the way that you feel is best for you and that you will leave if it no longer suits you to stay. You are never trapped. Only you can trap you in a situation or a conversation. You are never rude to express your willingness to leave, and maybe if you begin to leave, your friends and relatives will think before they speak.

Many of you deal with these fearful situations and the fear is based on guilt. The guilt comes from not liking the way a certain person responds or acts. This is okay. You do not have to like how everyone acts. Most of you are unhappy and acting it out in some way. So; when you see someone dump anger or strive for pity, I suggest you sit back out of the way and watch and learn. Why do they do it? What begins to set them off? How hard do they try before they lose it and get upset?

You are watching you. You all have your panic button or your short fuse, and some are shorter than others. What frightens you? Does it upset you when you don't receive due respect from others? Does it frighten you to know you didn't obey an authority (the judge, the boss, parents)? Why are you so afraid of authority? Did someone in an authority position abuse you? Was it a teacher, a baby-sitter, a parent, a police officer? You begin to fear others by being hurt in some way. Get to your hurt. You have all been hurt in some way and you are now protecting yourself from further abuse.

Do you find loud people offensive, yet you often raise your voice or maybe speak loudly? This too is fear. A raised voice is *screaming* to be heard. Maybe you sat and witnessed a fight and could not relay your feelings of confusion, so now you find you speak in a loud voice and often raise your voice louder than necessary. You are practicing what you were taught. If you saw toughness growing up you will be tough, or you will hate toughness so much that you will be weak and feel like others are bullying you by their authoritarian ways. They are not; you are just so terrified of bullies that you let everyone have their way, so they will leave you alone.

The only problem is that in giving in to others they will want more. So; what can you do when you find yourself in situations you do not appreciate? You may leave. You may simply say "I'm leaving now" and not even explain why. No explanations are ever necessary. You do not answer to others, you answer only to you and you are God. So, if God already knows why he or she is leaving, why would he or she expect an excuse? You are so programmed to be polite to others that you have forgotten to be polite to you. This is today's lesson. Do not '*fear*' fear. Go into your fears; and stand up tall and say "no thank you" if it does not feel good.

The more you go into your fears, be it climbing a mountain or facing the relatives, the more you may learn about you. It is not necessary to explain or make excuses for your behavior. You are doing for you, not for them. I know that you were taught to honor and respect others, but now I am teaching you to honor and respect you. Think of everyone as a small child. Most of them could not understand your reasons or excuses, even if you explained them. Do you feel intimidated by a small child who tells you what to do out of his bravado, or do you simply say, "Don't be silly, I'm the adult." I want you to respond similarly with others. Simply say, "Don't be silly, I'm me."

When you begin to know your own pain, you will know why you are angry. When you know why you are angry you will *release* anger. You will be so unafraid of your anger that you begin to allow it out.

Most of you do not know that you are angry, and to not know is to not know you. As you begin to know you, you begin to know all parts of you. Anger is a big part of your lives. You began to take on anger to allow yourselves room to breathe. You thought if you got angry, you could control others and create your own kind of peace and calm through control. What you learned is that peace and calm cannot be gained by controlling others, it can only be attained *within* the individual. So, all your efforts to control others to get what you want is a waste of time and energy, if your goal is inner peace. You may however, learn to keep things quiet around you and your immediate surroundings. This is simply peace and quiet for the moment and it takes some time convincing the others to be quiet and allow you peace.

If you truly want peace you will find it within. All joy comes from within and if you wait for someone else to create your joy, you must also wait for someone else to create your peace. No one is in charge of you but you. You are the one responsible for you. You are not responsible for the actions of another and you are not responsible for the pain of another. You must learn to be you and not try to be everyone else.

Begin by giving you credit where credit is due. If you are in a good place, you got you there. If you are in a mess, you got you there. Do not judge you for the bad stuff and not accept the good stuff. Begin to *accept* your good as good. Sometimes you simply do not *realize* how good your life is. Do not be afraid to accept the good. If you can allow the pain you can also allow the good. Do not limit your good by accepting it conditionally. In other words, don't limit your good by saying, "Yes, it is good *but* it could be better." Let your good stand on its own. Allow your good to be.

Allow your pain to be by accepting that part of you, and allow your good to be by accepting that part of you. You will learn that pain is not real and you will learn that peace of mind is simply a step in the right direction. That direction is *within.* Go within and know you so that you might accept you. Once you begin to accept you, you will find a way to be you. Once you give yourself permission to be who you are, you will no longer judge who you are.

Most of you are so caught up in judgment that you no longer realize who or what you are judging. You are not a victim of anyone or anything. You choose to stand where you stand and sit where you sit. You choose compromise at times and you choose debate and battle. All choices are made by you... some part of you, be it conscious or unconscious. You have decided, on some level, to stand up and fight or to lay down and submit. I am now asking you to turn and walk away. You need not fight and you need not submit. You need not even finish a discussion that is not going well. You may always leave. Someone taught you that you must listen to what everyone is saying and this is incorrect. You may get up and walk away and do not fear what they may think or say.

You have been taught to stay and listen out of respect for others' wishes and opinions. Now I want you to do out of respect for self and your own opinions. It is not taught to hit back, but you do. It is not taught to slander, but you do. It is not taught to debase, but you do. I now want you to teach yourself to walk away. Your natural instinct at this point is to fight and argue. That is what has been taught and ingrained in you. You see it all around you. You never see "them" leave without "them" being associated with cowards or weak people who cannot stand up for themselves. To stand up and walk out is okay. I give you my permission to stand up and walk out. Everything and every situation has a choice to offer and you may learn to make better choices by realizing that you have greater options.

Now; in the case of someone who is being held against their will, I suggest you seek assistance within. Find out why you chose this type of situation to learn from, and totally accept the situation. Remember; fear is not real and death is not a punishment. This alone will assist you in your dilemma.

You will find that you do not have to be alone to have fear. You can be in a very large loving family and be totally traumatized. It is all a matter of perception. You may perceive yourself as being un-accepting and unlovable.

This creates resistance wherever you go, simply because you cannot accept your lovability. As you begin to see how lovable you are, you will begin to see how love was always with you but you simply did not know how to receive it.

Now I wish you a good day in which to look for the good in yourself. You are good – you are God!

When you begin to know who you are and how you respond to fear, you will begin to know your own love. You will find that as you release fear, love moves in. As you begin to rise above your level of conscious thinking to a more acceptable level, you will accept love as your right. You will allow light to be and you will allow love to move you in a new direction.

Love is not only movable, love is flexible and love is constant. Love does not tie you down and love does not set you free. You set you free to be love. Love is not something to search for in order to be free. Love, like God, is constant and ongoing and expanding. Love allows all to exist and love allows all to be. Love is the beginning and the end. Without love you would not be, for love is what you are.

Desire is quite another idea altogether. Desire is the search for, the yearning for, the wanting of. To love is not to desire and to desire is not to love. So, if you are confused about loving someone and not wanting to let them go, this is not love. Love lets go. Love does not trap. Love does not make rules and love does not lose, because there is nothing to be lost. There only is love.

Let go of your fear of loss. Loss does not exist. All energy is continuous. It moves and grows and waits to be accepted. Love is not something you decide upon. You decide upon contracts and buying big houses and collecting debts, but you cannot decide to love. Love is you and is constant. You may love someone and never actually see or touch them because love is simply your acknowledgment that *that someone* is acceptable. You need not accept by definition of receiving. You receive only what you give and you give only what you have received.

More than anything love is creation, and if you receive creation you receive love. Love does not move and love is not fixed. It simply is. It takes up all space and time, and you either allow it in or you reject it. You may not *refuse love* and exist for long. Light, or love, is a necessary element of survival. You may shut everyone out of your life and still be love. People do not create love and people do not own love. You may simply love and accept nature, or you may simply accept and love you, or you may simply love and accept everyone and everything.

The only painful part of love is lack of love, or not opening to self-love. If you have pain, i.e., stress, upset, sadness, nervousness, loneliness, illness, accidents, unusual feelings of doom, you are not loving or accepting you. I wish you to begin to love and accept you. I am not focusing this information on your neighbors, as you have often done. You are constantly and repeatedly told to love others, and respect others, and treat them as you would treat yourself. And of course, since you don't care very much for most parts of you, how in the world can you care for most parts of others?

You have a chain reaction going on here. Love of self is so low on your priority list that you are creating a chain reaction outside of you, in your projected image. Life is not meant to be painful. Stop judging others by letting go of judgments against you for not doing good enough. You will find that when you no longer judge the self you will accept the self, and of course, when you accept the self you love the self.

Let go of this desire to be more than you are. You strive to be bigger and better and I want you to be smaller and less. You will find that less is actually a great deal more than you think. Do not strive to be acceptable by getting bigger and better; you are going the wrong direction. Come down off your high horse in order to rise above what you believe to be unacceptable. You will not lose you in this process of stepping down and becoming less. You will actually, finally have the time and the desire to relate only to you. You will finally have the time to get to know you, to go into you, to come out of "out there" and go "within."

You do not win big awards doing this "relationship with the self" work. You do, however, get to see the light, and oh... what a wondrous gift to actually *see the light!*

When you come to know God you will know who you are. Many of you are not interested in knowing God and you do not wish to spend time getting to know God. God is not important to you because you do not understand the God connection.

God is love and light, and love and light create. The creative force is love. Conception begins when you begin to conceive of an idea. Idea then springs forth and brings light with it. Idea is based on knowledge and knowledge comes from experience. Right now you are very limited in your knowledge. You know little and assume a lot. Most of you are not even aware that you are connected to God wisdom and knowledge. So, if you are connected, how is it that you do not know who you are and how you create? You have malfunctioned and need a good cleaning out. I am teaching you how to clean you out and reprogram your computer in order to end this computer virus that creates greater fear.

Your unintelligence is just a brief situation. Once you are cleaned up and put on the right track, you will do very well. Most of you are just stuck with gum and mire from past lives and childhood. I will get you unstuck if you will just begin to trust that you are connected to me. I am God. You are God. I wish to help you ascend by lifting your ideas, which create your world. You may live in a new world simply by seeing all differently.

Now; when it comes to pain and hurt, you are

being taught to accept it by admitting you have it. By admitting you have pain, you own all parts of you. When you see your pain for what it is, you may then acquire the necessary tools to work through your pain and allow it to change into something better... hopefully enlightenment!

Most of you have so much pain and you deny that you do, because you do not know that you do. So, why at this time am I teaching you to accept this part of you? Because there is no evil. You all believe in evil in some form and this is incorrect. Pain causes confusion and dysfunction. I don't care if it is in body or out of body pain. You may have emotional pain (energy) trapped in what you call a ghost. It is not exactly like your physical pain, but very close.

So; if pain is trapped in a human or a ghost, and pain is in control, how do you explain to that being, be it human or non, that he must change? You simply get him to admit he hurts. Get him to look at his own pain and he will begin to understand why he is aggressive and uncaring to others. It is his own aggressive anger at his own pain that drives him to harm others and frighten others. It is not his true identity. It is pain, causing turmoil.

I want you all to feel your pain, so you will have to admit that it is there, controlling your movements and the ease in which you might live your life. When you get to the bottom of your pain, you will know how much low self-esteem you carry. This is not to bring you down. This is only to show you part of you that you do not accept at this time. Most of you are in total denial of your pain because you are so afraid of pain. This is the best you can do from your level of intelligence. What I want you to do is to go beyond your current level of intelligence. Get in touch with all parts of you no matter how awful, or ugly, or nasty, or painful you think they may be. You must learn to accept *all* of you in order to become whole. You have been fragmented and in pain since the fall, and now it is time to rise up and become whole.

Come together within your own self. Know thy self. Know you and you know God. See you and you see the connection. Don't be afraid to look at your own messes, be they big or small, do not be afraid of what you, out of lack of awareness, may have given yourself. The experience of knowing is worth a thousand words. You can teach yourself to change your mind and to handle pain and hide pain, but I highly suggest you face your pain straight on and really feel it and experience it, so you can let it go. Just re-experiencing pain sends it off in a new channel of light.

You will not die from knowing all parts of you, but you will feel you change and stretch and grow. It may not feel good at first, but you will learn that you are just contacting and letting go of all the layers and layers of garbage that you have lived behind in order to feel safe from your own self. It is no longer a good idea to hide from God. You will learn to face your demons and not simply push them away as though they are separate from you.

The fear is a very real part of you, because you have made it real. Once you face your fears (your demons) you will be afraid of no one and nothing. It is all an illusion.

The fear is just attached to the pain and the pain created a need for protection. Once judgment leaves, there will be no more pain and no need of protection. Many of you are placed in an animated state of protection to get you started, as Liane was when she first began her books for God. Then, as you can handle it, you are given small, and sometimes large, doses of what you need to trigger your fears and get them up to the surface.

This process does not always feel good, but it is very effective. You have infection inside of you and I am forcing this infected area out into the open... up to the surface... into the light. This is how you will come to the light. You bring all parts of you up to the surface, so your own light might shine on them and heal them. Think of this as a summer vacation, where you take off your clothes and go to the beach so the sun might shine down on you and help heal your frazzled nerves. I am taking you out of you and into the light. This light will heal you. Please bring all parts of you. Do not fragment or deny any part of you.

When you begin to understand how you are all "one," you will begin to know more clearly who you are. You are not meant to be in pain and you are not meant to be in confusion. All pain centers around misunderstanding and confusion. Even when you have physical pain, it is centered around this confusion and misunderstanding. Without physical pain there would be no signal to the body to stop the abusive behavior causing the pain.

All abusive behavior is meant to be in a pattern, so it might be more readily accepted. This, of course, is according to how you divide and split your energy in order to handle the abuse. Once you begin to divide and split in order to handle pain, you create separation within the self. It begins like this; you hurt yourself and cause great emotional stress. You begin to freak out and so you shut it off for a while to go back and deal with it later. When you come back to it later, it appears to be okay, not so out of control, and you are grateful. The most interesting thing is that, once in a while, it (the turmoil you felt) may erupt again and again over small incidences that you are not really that upset about. The reason you are erupting over something small is because you were not healed from the original cause of your pain. You left it to heal itself and since you left it, it decided to create on its own. Now it does, and you go crazy at times over the smallest thing, but it is not small to you, it seems very big indeed.

This is retracing, or re-experiencing the original pain, without actually knowing it. The original pain must be dealt with before segregation ends. Integration will come when you can face the original cause of your original pain. This is why I have taken Liane *in* to see her hurt and pain. She was sexually abused and the remembrance of the original pain creates fear and mistrust of people, and she would not have known why she did not trust, or why she did not get married, or why she had such strict rules regarding her own sexual freedom. She not only did not trust men, she did not trust anyone, because some part of her who was never dealt with was so hurt and in fear that, that part of her controlled her life from the inside out. And of course, like you, she thought that this was just the way she was meant to be.

You are not meant to be alone and you are not meant to be separated form your own parts by fear and guilt and shame. You are meant to be whole. You are meant to be one. You are meant to be clean. Do not judge yourself as bad or dirty, no matter what you have done. Stop punishing you for creating pain for yourself and for others. Let go of pain by letting go of how you view you. Love you. Cherish you. Stop you from killing off parts of you that you judge as not good or too ugly. You are God in all his glory, and the only reason you do not believe this is because you are so full of self-judgment.

Be kind to yourself and allow yourself the freedom of acceptance. Accept you as you accept others. You allow people to lie and cheat and still you accept them. Why not allow you the same honor. Allow you to be innocent like you do with others. You have friends who are pretty messed up, but you accept them as they are. You simply say, "Oh that's just Uncle Charlie and that's the way he is," or, "Oh well, she's a good friend, I'll let her get away with a little lie. I know she's just protecting herself." You may accept you just as readily, and give you a break in the same way you give them a break.

Why do you have to live by such strict rules and not your friends? Oh, did you do something wrong so you must be punished, or is it maybe that you simply do not trust your own self, because you were bad or did something you believe to be wrong? It is for you to forgive you. It is not necessary for God to forgive you, as God never judged you. It is all up to you. It all begins and ends with you. You decide, as you always have.

When you begin to see the light, you will begin to see love. Light is love and light is you. You are the love and the light of this world. You will begin to know who you are when you begin to accept your own truth. Each time that you deny your truth you deny you. You are telling you that you do not live or that you do not exist, not as love and not as light.

This is a very difficult time for you, for you do not believe in you. You may believe in God and you may believe in others, but you do not believe in you. You are afraid to be alone with only you because you believe it will not be rewarding. So you surround yourself with those you believe to be special in hopes that you become special through them. You are not fair to you. You do not trust that you are the light of your life.

You believe you are nothing and you believe that without a particular job or title you will be unloved. You believe you need to be somebody in order to be accepted.

You believe that to "be without" is to be in trouble and you believe that to be alone is a bad thing. You do not need everyone's approval to know you are good! You are good by birth. You are good by having the courage to be here. You are good for being you, and you are good by being God. No one is here but you. You are not some small nothing of a person who must prove himself or herself. You came to be free, not to prove yourself. Stop proving how great you are by how big you become. Give it a rest. Goal setting is getting you deeper into matter. Come out of this illusion of material wealth and grandeur.

Kings and queens may fall, but love is constant. You don't become grand by how much you produce or how much you own. Stop being so materially productive and become spiritually productive. You become grand by the amount of light you see. How grand are you? How much light do you see? Where are you in you; not in riches, but in you? This is the true measure of self-worth. You are not so afraid to be alone as you are afraid to be you.

You are afraid you will be lost, and you can never be lost when you know you. Do not measure or recognize your abilities by the length of another. You are you. You are unique and you are very special; you have a plan. You came here with a plan and soon you will wake up enough to know what your plan is. It may be as simple as just smiling and enjoying this plane or it may be as big as writing books and teaching. Let the plan be – be it large or small, let it unfold. Who are you to judge why you are here and what you are learning.

Now; I realize how difficult it is to create from

poverty and to convince others that to not have is good, so I suggest you keep this to yourself for now. Money is only energy and it has no more power than any other energy, unless *you* give it more power by your thoughts regarding it. Prosperity is a whole new thing for you. Prosperity has little to do with money and a great deal to do with wealth and joy. So; begin to prosper by letting go of being responsible for so much material wealth and get down to spiritual wealth. *Spiritual wealth can be taken with you.*

You are now on your return trip. You are being rescued from your own creation. You will find that as you return you will become aware of parts of you that triggered problems for you. You will learn what triggers you and you will learn what makes you tick.

These are most wondrous times and they are yours for the exploration into self that is necessary to know self. You cannot know you without looking at you and you cannot look at you if you are busy looking outside of you. You spend the majority of your life trying to understand and dissect what is outside of you, when you could easily learn all by simply looking within.

Take the time to go within. Take the time to be alone with you. Take the time to know you. You are not so much an enigma as you are undiscovered. You are uncharted territory, and once you begin to explore you, you will know your every twist and turn. You will know what makes you angry and why. You will know what makes you hurt and why. Once you know what and why, you will begin to know how to change your programming from pain to joy and from anger to peace.

You will find that you are not so rigid that you cannot change, and you will find that change is all that really exists. In other words, you will learn to change your reality by letting go of your belief in pain. You will learn to suffer little and gain much. You will learn to rise above pain by putting yourself in a better position. Most of you draw pain out of a need for punishment. You feel the need to hurt yourself, so you turn any little thing into a big thing so you can feel hurt.

The best way to deal with pain is to let go entirely and allow all pain to simply be. See it as confusion and don't own it or take offense. A great deal of pain comes from taking offense at the words of another. You are hurt because he or she said this or did that. In such cases, your belief in punishment-of-self leads you to take this position of judgment in order to feel pain, as you have always believed in pain. Words cannot harm you and yet you *use* words to feel pain. You need pain. Pain is your punishment for being bad. You believe yourself to be a bad person, so you will create pain to punish you for your sins.

This was taught early on in life and has always been taught. Even in past lives you were taught punishment for being bad. No one punishes you as much as you punish you. You are so full of judgment and shame that you frequently create some new pain just to feel a jab here or there. You are not comfortable without pain as it is your friend. Pain has always been with you and pain is your dear friend. You trust you, only because you have pain as your friend to show you your limitations. If pain did not stop you, you would run amuck and enjoy too much!

Actually, pain had a very good place in creation at one time. Then you began to use pain in other ways and now, as most on your planet, pain is out of control. It is no longer a signal to tell you something is wrong. Now it is completely misused and totally misunderstood. So, let go of your belief in pain as a punishment. Use pain only to signal you that your leg is sore, or your arm is weak and exhausted and must rest. Do not use pain to get your way and do not use pain to gain dominance over another.

Use love and show love. Do not beat your children into submission. Do not treat them with disrespect. Allow all to be love. If you cannot control your children, allow them to move to someone who can and knows better techniques than beating. Yelling is okay; but remember that sound is vibration and not only do you affect those you yell at, you also affect vegetation and other life forms. If you must yell, I suggest you do it only in the medicinal sense of clearing trapped energy. Yell it out and vibrate it out. This type of yelling is not to be directed at a target – it is not abuse, it is release.

Allow all release to be made as a service to restoring perfect health. Sometimes the unhealed places have no release once they reach the surface. Allow all healing to occur. It is most important at this time to allow release, as the triggers are gaining in impact. Release of energy is necessary to provide balance during this *shift* in perception. As always, the most powerful form of releasing energy that is trapped in the body is enema. Use this technique, and release huge amounts of toxic waste and energy each time you do it.

You will find that you are not so afraid of releasing as you are afraid of knowing you and all that you contain. You will not "know you" by never touching, looking at, or feeling your body and your emotions. You are all connected to all parts of you and you cannot deny some and accept others. This is separation, it is not becoming whole. You are on a wondrous trip into you, and you may not care for all that you find, but you will learn to let go of what is not light and keep what is. This is transformation. This is darkness leaving and light entering. Darkness is simply confusion and light is simply enlightenment. Know that you are light and know that you are simply becoming more of what you are. You are no longer "dark" becoming more of what you were. You have "tuned in" and "turned on" the light. Good for you!

As you begin to wake up to your own ability to create, you will learn to create greater and greater gifts for yourself. The first step is to clean you out and reprogram you. You have been programmed for self-destruction by your belief that you are bad and now you must be programmed for love. You must learn to love you. You must focus on treating you like a real good friend.

This is to be done through an exchange of thought energy. You must change the way you see yourself. You must begin to change your own awareness and see only "love and light" in you. You must learn that you are the light and the love of God. You are very special and you are very, very much love. You are so much love that you would fall to your knees in adoration of you if I could just get you to see who you really are. You are the one who knows all and the one who is all. You are the great one who is coming. You are God in all his glory. Do not judge you as less than God. You are God and God is you. You are the prince of men and the king of life. You are the one who is here to save you from you, and you still don't recognize you. You will see you clearly when you learn who you are. When you have been reprogrammed and shown the truth, you will be amazed at the changes you begin to see in yourself and in all life.

You are so vast that you do not know how much of you even exists. How can one so great not realize his or her own ability to create? When you begin to know who you are you will begin to create out of love, not out of fear. Love will guide your every move and love will put you in your right place. As you begin to realize the importance of your move, you will know that you have always been in your right place. As you move closer to the light you will find it more and more intense. Therefore, you will move slowly and with caution. This is a new experience for you and you must not be in too big a rush. You might say that you are being acclimated to this new vision or view of you.

You will not begin to know you by never experiencing any of your emotions. So; if you find yourself going through difficult, emotionally upsetting times, I highly recommend relaxing and knowing that you are being *moved* (in the emotions) to a better place. You are being put in a position that you consider to be fearful so that your system might clear any charge it carries regarding these situations. It is similar to putting you back on your bike after your first big fall. You hurt yourself and now you think your bike is this big bad machine that is out to get you. If you don't look at it or touch it, it can't hurt you. But the truth is that you have created an irrational fear, out of a basic instinct to survive without pain.

If your parents are smart, they will coax you back up on your bike. You may fall a time or two, but you will eventually learn that your bike is no monster waiting to get you or hurt you. Your bike is just a machine that you learned to ride and now you are learning that *you* can create a good ride or a bad ride. You can create fun and games or emotional scarring. You create. There is no one else. If you hurt, you created it. If you are gun shy, you created it. If you are having fun, you created it; and if you are in emotional pain, you created it.

So now I must get you back up on your bike to show you this. It won't take long to get into the pain and trauma, but it may take awhile to clear it so you can come to the light. Please be patient as you clear emotional pain. It is important to release it all so you can move freely. It will take as long as it takes, and since there is no time it does not really matter. You may not like being held in place, but it is the best thing I can do for you at this time.

Since you believe in right and wrong and the realms of matter, I must work within these parameters. You will see no great change until you actually begin to release the belief in right and wrong. That is when you will begin to know who you are.

When you begin to learn about your own self-growth, you will know that you are not growing bigger, you are now growing smaller. It is no longer necessary to carry all that you have carried. You are putting down your weight in order to ascend. You are letting go of what you once believed was you, in order to rise to a new level of understanding and insight.

You are no longer the big dark hole. You are becoming light, and as you grow in light the entire universe will reflect your growth. You are no longer stuck. You are beginning to move upward. This is what you requested. You wanted to rise above your own level of existence to a higher level and so you are. You are moving and rising and getting *stretched* a little in the process. This stretching has to do with time continuum. There is no such thing as time.

And your body believes in time, so as you move out of time sequence, your body must shift. Your body may reflect where you are, by giving off symptoms that are coming up to the surface as you move through time.

You may experience strange new sleep patterns, and you may experience lack of energy and emotional trauma. All of this is part of letting go and moving upward. Some may even experience aging before they begin the reversal to youth. For each individual it is different. Each of you got here (to this point in time) in a different manner, so each will experience differently as you retreat from matter and go within.

You are being sent on a most wondrous journey and it will lead to heaven. Do not be afraid of a few symptoms. It takes some broken eggs to bake a cake and you are baking a very fine cake. This analogy may not suit you as you no longer eat eggs, but you get the idea. You are going to be a very grand specimen of God. You are God becoming God and you will soon know that you are. The creator is going to wake up to the fact that he is indeed the creator. This will assist you a great deal.

Have you ever seen someone who is unconscious, maybe a drunk? He stumbles, this way and that, and bumps into doors and tables, and knocks over furniture. In the morning you might point out the mess he created in his drunken stupor. He, of course, won't remember unless you jar his memory enough. I am jarring your memory. You are in a drunken stupor and creating from it. Stop creating unconsciously and begin to create from conscious knowledge. Know what you create and be certain it is what you really want. You may know if it is what you really want by turning it over to God and not getting too involved with the outcome.

When you turn it over to God, you will be turning it over to your own higher self; the part of you who knows what you are here for. All else is nonsense. All else is just distraction. Let it go to God. Let yourself flow as a bottle in a stream. I will guide you up against anything that will help you clear your fears, and I will guide you into the current when you are ready to move on. Give it over to God. Tell God everyday to take your life into his hands.

If you cannot freely and willingly do this each and every day, you will know that you do not trust God. And if you do not trust God, how can you ever trust you?

It is most remarkable to see you change. You begin by subtly waking and shifting. You then begin to judge until all judgment is gone. This is probably the most remarkable state of your clearing. You judge life with the intensity of a bulldozer. You simply begin to hate and judge everything around you because judgment is at its peak.

When judgment leaves you, you will feel much better. You will see how you do not need judgment to keep you safe. You will see how judgment has been misused, and you will see how judgment creates the bond to pain. As you begin to clear pain, you will find yourself also clearing judgment, as these two are connected. Once you learn to no longer use pain, you will no longer *need* judgment to stop you from hurting. You have turned judgment around so it now harms where it once had a very good purpose.

You could once judge the distance between two points and even judge the height of a mountain without pain. Now you judge everything from the point of perspective created by good and bad. If the distance from point "A" is greater to point "B" than you would like; this is now a bad thing. Usually, anything that takes more time is bad, things that take little or no time are good. This is your current judgment against time. This comes from impatience, which comes from anger and pain.

We all know that when you are in pain the last thing you want to do is wait in a long line. So, with pain, patience goes right out the window. This is also true of love. Love is absent when pain is in. You will find that, as you request to see your pain you will *feel* pain. This has two reasons. One: is that pain must be experienced through the emotional channel in order to become knowledge or wisdom learned, and two: pain is not dormant in you without you knowing it. And this part of you who knows you carry pain must now experience it, so you will cop to the truth that pain is hidden in you.

So, as you begin to rise up, you will feel the exact opposite of what you request until you are cleared and released of darkness. If you ask to be love and light, all of your dark and unloved places will come to the surface at some point. So, don't be discouraged or disgusted with yourself as you clear your unhealed places. Be patient and loving and kind to you. You are God's patient and he is doing a little bit of surgery on you. You will not feel his knife as he cuts you open to drain the wounds, but you will require rest and a good long healing period after surgery.

As each symptom leaves, it will leave an opening in you for light to come in and take over. Some spaces are being filled with light while still in the process of removing darkness. This often creates a battle within or Armageddon factor. You will feel this as pain, confusion, dizziness, and sometimes headaches. You will be experiencing the battle for the takeover between light and dark. Your two forces will be fighting it out and it is all within you. You are being converted to light. You are becoming God right in front of your very eyes and you don't realize it. You only feel pain and discomfort, and wonder why you are so confused. It is all to heal your wounds, it will not last forever. Please be patient and remember how long it took to get you this messed up. It is not only childhood trauma, it is also past lives. So; in one brief lifetime, you will heal the scars of millions of wounds from millions of battles. This is not to be taken literally, but you get the idea.

So; as you go forth on your journey into you, I wish you to be as easy as possible with you. Be gentle and kind and do not judge you too harshly. After all, you are creating God out of you!

When you begin to receive light, you will find that you no longer wish to be dark. It may be difficult at times, but this process of ascension will be most rewarding. You will find that awareness has its own rewards and you will wish to remain awake and not return to your former unconscious state. One of the rewards of awareness is the ability to see situations as helpful instead of harmful. As you wake up you will see "all" through awareness.

If someone does not agree with you, you will see this situation more clearly by estimating your ability to understand this disagreement. In most cases it is a gift. Do you wish to change everyone's mind about you or do you wish to know right up front if you are compatible? It is really this simple. You may feel hurt and rejected by them now, but as you learn awareness you will see the gift is being "assessed" and put-in-place right up front. This actually saves you time, energy, and confusion.

So; when you learn rather abruptly that you are headed in a completely different direction than those you associate with, this is actually good. It is quicker and safer to learn right up front. You save time and thought and confusion. Get your answers and know your right place. You are each being moved to your right place and you do not necessarily go "together" to your beginning position. Some of you must separate in order to come into position. Allow yourself to let go of anyone you are holding on to for your safety. You fear being alone so you attach yourself to another. Let go!

You must learn to stand on your own with no fear. If you cannot stand on your own you are leaning on others for your security. I wish you to lean on God. How can your security and trust be based in your own God-self when you are busy trusting someone else to keep you safe and secure? You are the one who is you. Do not try to make someone else responsible for you. You are not alone. You are so multidimensional that you may never know all of you. Stop attaching yourself to those outside of you and begin to go within to those who are you.

You are not in this alone. You have never been alone, and you may never be alone, if you only choose to look at all of you. When you begin to look at you, you will know how you are multidimensional and you will be amazed at how many parts of you that you are totally unaware of. You may think you are not. You may hate what you see in someone else only to discover that you judge that very thing within your own self. You are not to be so hard on yourself when you discover these denied parts. Most of what you are discovering is confusion, and confusion is darkness. You are looking at your dark places in order to shine your light on them. In the light they may heal. In the light they do not belong hidden, they belong to you. When you own them, you may heal them. If you do not see these parts of you, you will not know who and what you are made of.

You have many layers and you are peeling these layers to remove the old crusted way of believing. Thoughts create, and you have many layers of encrusted old memory belief that must be changed. It will change by transforming it to light energy. All, absolutely all, is to become light!

As you begin to move to your right place, you will feel torn. You have been stuck in one position or one way of seeing an issue for a long time and this often creates rust. You are rusty! You do not know how to be flexible. You are old rusted thought and we are now oiling you up to make you move.

You will see that all is not as you once thought it was. You will also see that all is not lost. You are gaining by moving. You are gaining by letting go and giving up. You are not so much in a position to see this at this point in time. You, however, have a great deal to learn regarding you.

You are still very strong in the will, and this breakdown of will motivation to spiritual motivation will take some time. It is not so much that you are being led around by "your nose," as you are being led around by "will power." You will give up will power for soul power. You need only let go of your "will to compete," and your "will to be as good as," and your "will to be stronger than," and "better than," and "bigger than," and "bolder than." Just be you. Accept you as you are.

You are not so low on the scheme of things, as you believe. You are not so bad that you must push at others to show off your strength. Stop pushing. Leave them be. You are you and you need not prove who you are. You are acceptable to God, why worry about being acceptable to others? You will find that it is 'not' often a lonely path to being you. It is simply *your path*. You are the one walking your path and you need not force others to come with you out of your fear of loneliness. Walk your path and live your life. Do not attach to others for support. Allow you to be alone. Alone is not bad. You never really are alone anyway.

You are love and light! You light up your own life. You need no one else to do it for you. You light your own way. I am here with you. I am you. Do not lean on others for support. Lean only on God. God is your best friend. God is you. You are your best friend. Stop beating you up with your judgments, and begin to enjoy your best friend.

There is no good way to show you how you will ascend. Ascension is basically moving from one level to the next. Each time you move upward in thought you actually take a step toward ascension. You are not so stuck that you cannot move your thoughts. You must learn to adjust your thinking to a level of awareness that allows for freedom of movement.

When you are free you are actually flexible to do your own work. When you are flexible you are like putty in my hands. As you become free you will "feel" this freedom within yourself. It is like looking at a whole new point of view. It is like being stuck in something and suddenly being released. It is like seeing life for the first time without any harsh judgments toward it. Life is not so painful as you believe. It is all what you have made of it, and what you have made of it is represented by the layers and layers of past life programming.

You are entering a new era and this new era is most becoming for its point of perspective. This era will be with you for some time and it will assist you in your rise. You each have your own "idea" of what heaven should be and you often are so "attached" to this idea that the truth is pushed away. Heaven is actually a way of life. It is an awareness and enlightening state. You will not find your heaven in the material world. You must seek joy outside of the material. The material plane is just there to play with. It is not the beginning and the end. It does not bring everlasting joy.

If you are looking for peace, joy, contentment and light, I highly suggest you ask for these. Most of you ask for money, cars, houses, trips, whatever material wealth you believe will get you to your goal, which is usually peace – peace of mind as well as peace within. Do not focus on the new car, or the big house, or the great job, or the big win. If you want peace, focus on peace within you.

Did you ever notice how some can have so much and still be so miserable? Yes, money pays the bills and eliminates fear to a great extent, but you also create your situations, and sometimes there is a big gift in losing your house or your job. Sounds pretty awful doesn't it? This is your fear of loss speaking. If you lose your house you will always find a way. You are resourceful. You are creative. You are God. You cannot 'not' trust in you. This is what destroys you.

You are the ever-living, everlasting God and you only think of yourself as vulnerable, and painfully and easily punished. Stop thinking in these terms. There is a reason for everything and it has little to do with punishing or hurting you. It has a great deal to do with setting your spirit free. Trust these times. They are the best of times; they are the worst of times. You choose how you will see them.

So far you do not believe you are different than you were when you began to read this series of books, but you are. Insight gives you new thought idea and new thought idea creates whole new realities. Your thoughts and beliefs will change enough to change your entire reality, for your reality is based solely on what you believe to be true. You are being moved in a direction that will assist you in your ascension, in your rise to the top. You are being put in a position that will assist you, and you are being put in a position that requires a great deal of movement. After all, how can you get from point A to point B without movement?

When you begin this movement, you will feel pulled at and stretched, and sometimes you may feel forced into or out of situations. You are not experiencing difficulties so much as you are experiencing change. Change is good. Change is what you are here for. You have no great reason for being in this plane other than simply passing through. So, if you are just passing through then I suggest you let go of your attachments and pass on through. Don't be tied to this or that. Allow everything to be as it is and allow everything to move at its own pace. Do not force your will on others and do not force others to submit to your wishes. You are here to learn for you, not to learn how to make others "be."

You are ascending for you, not for them. You are rising at your own pace and you need not concern yourself with the others and their pace. You will experience whatever you need in order to change you, not them. Avoid your lessons if you wish and you will still learn and grow. You cannot 'not' grow. It is impossible to not grow. You are at a time of fast paced growth and vital need for thought to shift. Your thoughts must find the direction to your own destiny. Your thoughts will lead you home to God. Your thoughts will lead you inward to your own God-self. Your thoughts are who you really are. Without thought you are not.

There is no "bad" thought. There only is thought. Thought projects outward and returns. You are God's thoughts projected "outward" and now you are returning.

You do not stay. You did not go there to stay. You went to explore, not to stay. You have a place to stay already and that place is within God. Do not judge those who look different or think different. The ones who are most unusual and different are moving at the greatest speed. They are changing by not being normal and easily adaptable.

It is not so much that they do not fit in, as it is that they do not ride the same wave or walk the same path. They are not afraid to 'not' conform, or not do as the crowd, or the majority. You are all making changes in some area. Watch your thoughts create for you. Do you like what you see? Does it feel good to you on some level? Are you moving or are you stagnant? You will find that those who do not wish to change will be allowed to sleep for as long as it takes. Each of you will be allowed your own pace.

The most important drive of ascension is the will to ascend. Now that you have come to a point of being movable and pliable, you will see great changes occur in you. You will see how you create and you will begin to *allow* the creation process without judging it or trying to block it. You are now on your way to consciously creating your own reality. Now you will see how and why this or that occurs. You will accept your world and you will know that you are just here for a brief stay in order to *pass through* to the next level.

As far as you go, you will not know you until you truly look at all of you. You are not alone and you are not meant to be. You are here to serve God. You are here as part of God to represent the coming of God. God does not represent love. God does not represent anything. God *is* all. He does not assume that you will do this or that, he simply *allows* you to do whatever it takes to get you back.

You have stepped out into the abyss and you are learning how to return. You are being pulled back, and you will feel this pull as stretching and pain. It will be seen as physical, mental and emotional pain. You are believing in all the wrong things and you must return to truth. The truth is, of course, that there is no wrong thing and that is how I will heal you. You will heal by not judging you for being you.

Have you ever noticed how bored you get when I repeatedly talk about healing you? You do not take much interest *in* you. You focus all of your attention outside of yourself and I want to bring your attention back to you, not your friends, not your lover, not your relatives, but you. You must learn to focus on you. You are the one who is here. They are not real. They are your projected images. You are not outside of you so why focus your attention outside of you. You get nothing from outside of you. All comes from within.

So – how do I get you to see this? I will tell you a story. Once upon a time a traveler came to earth. This traveler was just passing through. When he got to earth, he noticed it was a hostile environment, but that did not affect him because he was just passing through.

Then one day he met a very lovely lady who seemed to have a problem. She wished to avoid the conflict and hostility of her planet. He thought, "Oh boy, she is like me. Perhaps she came from far away and is searching for peace in all this conflict as I am."

So now the traveler began to assist this lovely lady. He forgot that he was just "passing through" and he began to coach her on the rules of peace and conflict. The more he coached, the more he learned about dealing with life on this plane. The more he learned, the more conflict he felt regarding truth and what he was now hearing.

In the end, the confusion of the conflict was so strong that he began to wander in order to find his own truth again. Truth can change, you know? It is very subjective, and once you create conflict out of two truths you are doing battle, and battle keeps you locked in and you are no longer simply passing through.

The irony of this entire situation is that due to the force of conflict that surrounds earth, the traveler picked up or magnetized an "image" who would "support" his belief that this plane needed help. So, of course, he drew an image who said, "Help me." And now he wanders not knowing how to get back to just passing through dimensions. You see; he is stuck to the conflict in his own mind. And until he lets go to simply "pass through" without any attachment to any reality or truth, he will remain stuck.

Let go my children. Stop believing in right and wrong. Let it all be. Why get involved in what does not concern you. If it is not inside of you, it does not concern you. You are simply passing through!

When you begin to rise up, you will begin to know no boundaries. You will become as a boundless spirit. You will lose all fear and know only freedom of expression and movement. As you rise, you will find it easier and easier to be joyful, for joy will come easily, and peace of mind will be yours.

You are now beginning this rise and you are now beginning to see how you can trust God and learn to know God. As you move from trust to faith, you will become absorbed in a state of eternal grace. This state of grace will reflect itself as pure joy and happiness. This is no joke. Once your mind is cleared of past debris that is clogging your circuits, you will rise. This is not to say you literally rise up off the ground… yet!

Some of you will literally rise up off the ground and this will be quite joyous for you. You will come to this point in your evolution as soon as you have cleaned you out and cleared your circuits enough to realize your potential and rise to your correct level of administration. You are no longer stuck in matter when you begin this type of strategy. You are only just beginning now to learn all of your potential. As you rise you will see more and more clearly how you manifest your own situation, and then you create from this manifestation.

It is much like rising above a situation that is chaotic, you see this chaotic situation and you wish to avoid it, so you project yourself into an area that contains only peace. This area may be literally peaceful, or simply a mental space for you to inhabit long enough to move through this chaos. Remember; you are just passing through! So now, this situation of chaos has been avoided simply by you rising above it and not getting involved or stuck to it. This is how I wish you to handle all chaos. Know it for what it is, but do not play in it. Do not act it out, for when you do you get stuck to it.

So, as you go about your daily lives, you may ascend a little each time you avoid getting hooked into a situation or involved in a situation that does not feel good. Allow all to occur, but if it does not suit you and you do not wish to wear it, leave it alone. Do not touch it if you do not want it to become a part of you. Wear only what you believe to be best for you. I would highly suggest peace. Peace is a very good vibration to wear. Do not live in chaos when you can live in peace. Do not force others to change just so you might find peace. If the situation at your home is not a peaceful one then I highly suggest that you leave. Go where there is peace or you will spend all your time creating more chaos by trying to stop the chaos. Move; leave; know your right place!

You would never leave a small child in the middle

of chaos or a battle zone, so why leave you in such a situation? Be kind to you. Love you enough to take real good care of you. You spend half your life searching for a mate who will fulfill your needs and care for you. You are your own creator and caretaker. Do not entrust you to another for safe keeping, and then get upset when the one you handed you over to does not take good loving care of you. You must begin to take good loving care of your own God-self. When you do, you will begin to see how easy it is to get along with others, because you will no longer expect them to act a certain way. They will have already been cued by you to know that you know you, and you care for you, therefore you have no expectations of them.

This lets them off the hook and puts you in charge of you, and they will comply with your choice in this matter, as they will see how you *need* no one but you.

When you begin to know who you are you will know love. You will know peace and you will know joy. Love does not bring peace and joy, but you will see peace just by accepting love. Peace comes in when conflict leaves. All conflict is within. Once you enter your inner being you must accept your conflict in order to raise its level of creation. You must look you squarely in the face and accept and acknowledge what you have done. This is much like an alcoholic who must first admit to his alcoholism before he may begin to heal. You are all addicted to something or someone. It is all right to know your addictions and dependencies. Only in knowing them and facing them can you learn to live without them.

You need no one. This is a grave misconception on this planet. All is there for your use, but you need no one. All that is needed has already been provided within you. You do not need to depend on another. Even a small child can learn to provide for him or her self. You are taught to not provide for yourselves. You are taught to depend on others for your needs. I wish you to bring all your needs to yourself.

You take care of you. You learn to love you. You learn to nurture you. You believe that without others you will die because you have taught interdependence on one another. I wish your dependence to be based on your own God-self. You need not be so afraid to "stand alone." You began to create huge societies to reinforce your belief that you must receive support from outside of your own self. There are no needs that cannot be met by you yourself. You will find that often you rely on others and depend on others, this is okay. Do not allow others to become a necessity. You do not *need* others to care for you. You are here to learn to be God in matter. You are not here to allow this field of matter to take over.

You give your power over to everyone and everything – drugs, alcohol, people, government, clothes, cars, tools, you become addicted to the strangest things. You are trying to fulfill a need in you. Find out what is out of balance in you and you will stop pushing outside of you to receive it. Remember; it all comes from within and sends messages out onto your projection screen. You are the projector, not the projection.

I will allow you to see only what you are capable of accepting at this point. If you do not wish to accept yourself and care for yourself, you will be permitted to continue handing your needs and wants over to someone else. This is how we work in this class – I tell you how it is and you continue on your merry way with your addictions and your abusive behavior. The nice part is, that once in a great while you put down your abusive ways and listen, really listen.

Now, I want you to realize that cigarettes and alcohol and drugs are just one form of abusive behavior. There are many ways of abusing you and you are a master at it!

As long as you believe that you require support outside of yourself, you will. When you begin to know that you are simply here to pass through and return, you will no longer be attached to people, places or things. You must learn to flow, to see all as being part of a big movie that you are observing. When you learn to watch and observe, you will learn to not get involved or attached to. The more you remain uninvolved or unattached, the easier it will be to *move* you to the light.

It's really quite simple; if you put down roots, you must be pulled up by your roots in order to move. If you have no roots, you are very easily moved. It is not a matter of not giving to the self and not enjoying at great length. It is rather a matter of enjoying everything without attachment to any of it. When you can learn to "love and accept," without holding on to or attaching to, you will be free; free of restrictions and free of entanglements. The freer you are the easier you move. To rise you must move. Move up in your thoughts and beliefs. Rise above this current level of seeing all. Be you by being free-flowing spirit in matter. Right now you are spirit stuck in matter. I wish you to change your position, I wish you to let all flow so that you might flow.

You are not so much stuck in matter as you are stuck in your own ability to transcend matter. When you begin to get your own awareness of who and what you are, you will no longer deny your own unique ability to rise above any given situation. All limitations are illusion, and when you learn to be who you are you will know this truth. For now, I suggest you allow your life to flow. See what comes to view on your picture screen and don't get involved, simply view it. Become the observer instead of the actor. Get out of these false roles that you play. Start by allowing everything to be, even the things you consider distasteful. Get out of their way, or step aside if something unpleasant should come at you, but remember that it is all illusion and you are ducking imaginary bullets, so don't get upset with the gunman.

You can do this. You can create a world of passive peace and calm. You once created a world of chaos and anger; so a world of peace of mind and calm should be very easy… don't you think?

*M*ost often you find it necessary to harm yourself in some way. This is due to judgment which creates a belief in punishment. When all judgment has left there will be no more punishment, be it self-punishment or the punishment of others.

Punishment is based on the need for revenge to keep the self or another under control. You see; as you begin to rise above your current level of intelligence, you will become aware of an intelligent choice, which is "it is no longer necessary to create pain in order to control." As you begin to exercise this new choice, you will create joy where once you created pain.

I will give you an example. Once upon a time a very young man decided it was not good to depend on others. He felt that if he depended on others he would be disappointed. He had spent his childhood depending on those who raised him and they only showed him neglect and unkindness. Now that he was a young man his choice was to lean only on himself. He began to care for himself in the only way he knew how. And of course, "the way he knew how" had been taught to him by his neglectful and unkind parents.

So now, he began to remind himself not to do as they had done. Anything they had done became a bad thing and anything new was acceptable. The only problem with his thinking is, he has just created great rules of right and wrong, or good and bad, for him to live by. Now when he breaks one of his own rules and crosses over into "their way" of raising him, he must find a way to bring himself back to his new good way of doing things. His best answer for this is to punish himself for doing as they did, for he now truly believes that what they did was wrong.

Now he decides that wrong deserves punishment because wrong created his pain in the first place. So each time that he does wrong, he chastises himself and swears to do better next time. Only, next time he forgets and slips back into what he was taught by his unkind, unloving parents, and so he chastises himself again and again, and before you know it he has become unkind and unloving toward himself. He is now punishing his own self for not being good enough.

You are good enough! Stop judging and you will stop punishing. Judgment is at the head of pain and punishment. All pain and punishment inflicted on self or on others is pushed out by judgment, or a belief in good or bad. Let go of good or bad. No good comes from being only one way. Allow all to be okay, for all is okay in the eyes of God. No one must ever be hurt in the name of good. That belief is sheer nonsense. Only allow all to occur and you are allowing God to choose for you.

You will find that you no longer wish to be caught in the tug-of-war game that you play with yourself. You are no longer so afraid to be you and yet you are still afraid to be you. This creates conflict. You have been taught to deny you and now you are coming out of denial. You are not who you wish to be. You wish to be God as you all know that you are, but you are afraid to act like you are. After all, it might not look "good" and "what will everyone think" and "how can accepting *all* possibly be good when we all believe in good vs. evil?"

You will find that good does not fight against evil. You make it so. You conflict and you fight and you create. This is your creation. This is what occurs inside of each of you and is projected outward. It is not bad, it is simply what is. Everything simply is. Get this part of your belief system clear and your life will change tremendously. You are simply changing your mind and achieving a higher thought pattern. You are raising your intelligence by raising your awareness. You are vibrating, and spinning, and moving, and creating a whole, new world, created out of awareness and acceptance... can you accept it? If you can accept it, you can live in it. If not, you will stay in your current housing.

This house is being raised for those who wish to move in. Others will find it necessary to build their own structure to live in. Your world, as always, is created by you and for you. Your choice is your choice and has nothing to do with your moving into Godhood. Godhood is achieved by each individual in his or her own time. This is not a race; it is simply a course in rising up.

You will find that you do not exactly know how to "rise above" until you let go of your anchor weights. Your weights are right and wrong. Let them go and you will lift off and on and up. You will find it easy to rise. It is so natural. It takes extra effort to stay down, and lots of control. To rise up you simply "let go."

When you begin to see how easy it is to not get involved, you will wish to know how to be love. You will wish to be love and light and God. As you get uninvolved, I wish you to remember who you are. You are doing this for you, not against anyone. You are becoming God. God does not attach himself to results and God does not lean on others for support. God allows all to occur and has no attachment to how things occur.

God does not rise up and stand or lord over others. He simply wishes to be. He does not wish to be born in accordance with man's laws. God is God unto himself, and God has little to do with man's laws and man's truth. God is truth in and of himself. He does not bow down to accept and he does not rise above to ignore. He simply is. God is love. God is forgiveness. God is light. God does not love, he does not forgive and he does not shine, for he *is* love, light and forgiveness. He is not the one who created heaven and earth. You created heaven and earth. You created all of this out of your need to explore and your need to become more.

Your expansion within yourself pushed outward and this is the result. This is not the cause; this is simply the effect. You are not the only creator and you are not the only one who is unaware of your Godhood. You are, however, very deep in your denial of self. You must first come out of your layering, then you must come out of your sleep. This is the process you are going to undertake. You are going to become more of who you are by becoming less of what you think you are. As you become less of what you think you are, you will feel as though you are losing. You are. You are losing the dense part of you. You are peeling away at you by bits and pieces. Do you feel like you are falling apart? You probably are.

The reason you will feel as though you are falling apart is that pieces of you are de-densifying and leaving. You are becoming lighter from a spiritual level, a mental level, and of course your body level. The mind is in the body. The cellular memory is within each individual cell, so of course you will feel this as a loss of energy. You are losing dense energy to replace it with light energy.

Now; as you go along you will feel a greater need to hold on to something for dear life. You may latch on to a particular life pattern, or a person, or number of persons, but in the end you will be standing alone and quite tall. You will be your own strength and you will no longer feel the need to draw on others for strength. You will be God. God draws on God. God does not use everyone else's strength.

Most of you search for a mate so you will have a partner to lean on. You do not so much search out of "love for," but you search out of *need.* This is what I wish to change. You do not know true love. When you learn to reach inside yourself to fulfill your needs and wants, you will no longer search for the perfect mate to fill up your missing parts. You will find that a mate will be very helpful in teaching yourself as to who and what you are. A mate will reflect back to you who you are. If you are unhappy with your mate, look at you not him or her.

Now; when it comes to twin soul mates, I wish you to know that you made an agreement because you wished to arrive at this point in time together, not to lean on one another as you on earth believe, but to reflect for one another. When you come into the life of a soul mate and you reflect their own essence right back to them, you *assist* them in their awakening process. This, of course, has little to do with sex and a great deal to do with love. On the higher planes love is not seen as attachment or sexual preference, as it is here on earth. On the higher planes love simply is. Love assists whenever invited to do so and love is the foundation of creation, so of course, love is interested in all creation. Love is God. God is love. God is the force or source of all and God assists.

Now; when you love someone you usually do not care about their faults because love is unconditional. You do not judge and you do not reject, you simply allow them to be who they are. You may even go on your merry way. To love someone you need not be actively involved with them. This is all a misconception of terms. You think that if you love someone you must be attached to them in some way. This is incorrect. Love is setting them free. They will stay if they feel true love because true love feels very, very good.

If you do not believe you are in love and you stay, out of guilt, you are not being loving you are being guilty. Do not love and move in guilt. Be love and be light. Light is knowledge and wisdom. Feel from light and awareness, not from fear and loss. You all must learn to rise above your fears. As you begin to rise above your fears, you will begin to know the truth. And the truth is "you are love" therefore you are never without love. Do not fear standing alone within yourself. You are self-contained. You are all that is here. All that you see outside of you is illusion. Stop reaching into the illusion to fulfill yourself. You are your source of fulfillment.

For such a long time you have been stuck in one way of seeing creation. You have come from one point of view and now you are being allowed to view the other side of the coin. You are not so misunderstood and ignorant that you cannot handle what you see without pain. You have achieved a certain level in this class and you are now capable (if you choose) to see the good in all. You know how this creation works and how you are best meant to perceive what you see.

Do not judge! If I could get you to do this one thing, I could free you. You are only caught in this cycle of distress by your belief in good vs. bad. If I can get you to let go of what you call bad… can you remember how sinful and distasteful it was just a few short years ago for a woman to smoke or wear a skirt above her ankles? She was labeled a harlot. You have stupid rules and they come out of ignorance.

You are superstitious and you have your rules to keep everyone under control. I know that you think you are progressive and intellectually motivated, but you are not. You are fear motivated and fear dependent. You look to your fear of not being in control to show you how to run your lives. It is so silly to watch. You no longer burn witches at the stake, but you chastise and criticize those who think or believe differently. You want all to be afraid of what you are afraid of, so that everyone will assist you in controlling and fixing things that you believe are wrong or bad. If you keep everyone here in the fear with you, you will never get up out of the fear.

Your rituals and rules and beliefs are now bigger than you are and they are controlling you. You feel unsafe because your own beliefs are attacking you. Your own threats are coming back at you. Begin to see how ridiculous this pattern is. You are not here to control or to change things. You are here to change *you*, and anything connected to you will automatically change in the process. Come out of the exterior expression of life and move into the self that is within you.

When you begin to focus on who you are and how you operate to create for or against your own self, you will begin to know you. Your own inner workings are the workings of your current creator. So; what are you creating and how does it feel to live in your creation? If it is less than wonderful I highly suggest you begin to change. Start with something very easy to do… do not get involved with creation; only observe each occurrence during this day. Do not judge it as good or bad. Just watch it and let it be. You need not get involved. Pretend that it is a dream and is not really happening at all.

*I*t is good to know that you do not die. It is good to know that death is illusion. It is good to know that pain is for your own defense against harming your own body. It is good to know that you are afraid to love out of ignorance and it is good to know that you are good. I am not teaching you anything that is not good for you. You only perceive information as bad when you believe it to be harmful. You are afraid of new information and you are afraid of new ways of viewing your reality. You are afraid of your own responses and you are afraid of the responses of others.

You will find that, as you grow into this new reality that you are creating out of trust and faith, your rewards on the spiritual level will be great. You will have no need for fear any longer. You have become addicted to fear and you are no longer able to see through the fear. It is similar to being addicted to drugs and unable to see clearly because you are in a drugged state. As you come out of this drugged state you will feel a little uncomfortable at first. You are accustomed to the feeling of being drugged and to be conscious is a little different.

You will feel a little uncertain as to who you are and even how you should act. This is all part of this process of taking off your layers and becoming less of what you were, in order to become more of what you are becoming. As long as you hold on to old parts of you, you are going to hold on to old beliefs and old programming. As you begin to let go, you may find that you no longer wish to be this new enlightened you. Most of you may experience pangs of wanting to return to the old you. You may feel safer being the old you, because you knew your boundaries and your limitations. However, the old you is literally gone, transformed by the light into this new you that you are experiencing.

This new you is not bad. This new you is simply different than your old limited self. You may fear that this new you is out of control or has no goals or is not restricted to answer to your will power, and this may be true. Your fear of no limitation may be the greatest fear of all. You fear not having limitations because you fear your own vastness. You fear being unlimited and you fear being God. Basically, you fear just about every part of your true identity. So, why do you become what you fear? Because you are light? You are not fear and fear does not rule.

You will drop your fears and you will become what you believe to be most dangerous. You will become light. You will become total love and acceptance of absolutely everything that is. It is so easy to be God. It is as easy and comfortable as taking off your clothes. You take off all that is burying you and you have what is left… pure light! You are in a state of transformation at this moment. Your pain will leave and your truth will stay. You need not layer yourself with locks and chains of limitation. You are a spirit who is made of light. You dance and sing without effort because spirit is life, and life is spirit. Spirit never dies and spirit never leaves.

You are in the process of uncovering buried treasure and it may take you a while to adjust to being the wealthy treasure owner that you are. There is so much *more* than the material world. Please begin to see how you are being transformed and brought forward into consciousness. It is not good to sleep through your own birth, only in that you will miss out on transformation. So come on now, wake up. See the light!

*S*o long as you know you are God, you will rise. You will always achieve greater standing simply by knowing who you are. You will not give up on you because you know you. When you begin to ascend to this new level, you will become lighter and lighter. You will become so light that you literally transform to light particles. As you achieve this level of ascended glory, you will know you no longer belong to earth. You will know you are not matter but that you are light. As you grow to this level of transformation you will no longer care how you look or appear to others. You will have become light – and light moves directly to God.

As light grows and works within you, you will feel the need to balance. You have been material density for some time and now you are changing to light. Your spirit or soul will vibrate within you and it will raise your level of conscious behavior back to God. You are not simply taking your spirit back to God you are taking all of you back to God. This is achieved by transforming all parts of you into light vibration. You need not slough off parts of you or leave parts of you behind.

Look at all parts of you, and begin to accept all parts of you. Do not judge what you see. You are being taught to accept you and to know you. Do not be afraid of you. You are being shown how you judge you so that you will let go of judgment. There is no right or wrong. There is choice. Any choice you make is okay. Any choice you make is good. Any choice you make is what you become. You will become your choices and your choices will show you who you are. If a choice shows you more about yourself, how can it possibly be bad? Every choice has a gift. Look for your gifts. You will know you by looking at your life and not comparing it to others.

If you compare, you are not accepting, you are competing, If you are competing, you are judging. How can life be built on judgment? Most judgment is created outside of the self and distracts the self from its true identity. Most of you live outside the self in competition. I wish you to come back to being *one*. Stay within you. *All* is within you. Do not merge into what he thinks or she thinks. Use your own guidance and intuition. Do not compete over who is closer to God or who is closer to truth. Simply be God. Know God. See God. You are God. Accept your own oneness with God by rising above your current level of belief.

You can do this. It is not so hard as you believe to just simply "let go" and not care who is right and who is wrong. You were programmed to function in this manner and now I wish you to function from truth and love and light. You will find that you are not so afraid as you believe. You will find that you will actually be relieved to join and become whole. Duality was never meant to rule and is virtually nonexistent in other planes of creation. Only you hold so tightly to your dual personality of good vs. evil. You do not want to give up or give in to what you call evil, so you force everyone to follow rules of good behavior to avoid evil behavior.

The only reason you have so much evil on this planet is because you call it evil. It is not evil. It is pain energy. It is sickness of the mind, sickness of the soul and sickness of the weak. The only reason you call it evil is because you are not insightful and intuitive enough to understand what is really happening on your plane. Rise above your current way of seeing life and you will create a more loving peace-filled life, without the need for evil or any other judgment call.

You will find that as you rise you will become less and less concerned with the evil atrocities of life. You will simply rise above this level of thinking and viewing. You will not be becoming a cold unfeeling individual, you will be becoming an enlightened observer who is *aware* that death does not really occur and therefore how can life have atrocities in the first place? You will know that you are simply the observer who is passing through and not attached to this dream.

So far it has been a very good class. None of you are too upset by my teachings and none of you wishes to hurt me for telling you the truth. This is very good. Usually you do not like to hear that you are not perfect and you often get your back up and begin to roar. This, of course, is due to all that programming that teaches you to be acceptable by doing the *right* thing.

As you move along you will find that you will have no need to rebel, for you will not feel confined or controlled. You will only feel love and acceptance because you will be loving and accepting you, and once you do you will have peace. You will draw only peace because you have peace *within.* Did you ever notice two children playing war and disagreeing on strategy and defense issues? You may watch them play this game, but you *know* that the guns are not real and the death scene is simply a stage play, and no one really gets hurt so why get involved? Let the children play their games and work out their emotions and develop into their own personality. This is how all life is played out. See it as children playing games. It is okay. No one ever dies. What are you getting so upset about?

You will find that to "live and let live" is a very good place to start. If you are pushing at someone to be better and it does not feel good, I suggest you stop. If you are creating chaos and it does not feel good, simply stop. If you are not feeling good and others are attacking you… leave. There are no set rules. Simply move over to a place that feels better, and by all means do not be afraid to move. Movement creates growth and gets you out of your stagnation.

So, if you wish to change the world, do not change everyone outside of you, change only you. Do not become afraid of living and experiencing simply because bullets are flying and you may or may not get hit. You will find that you will create in your outer world whatever you fear from within. If you fear war, you will create war, be it within you or outside of you. You cannot 'not' draw what you are. It is virtually impossible to simply stifle what you fear because sooner or later it will erupt in you. You will be forced to face all of you at some point because to love yourself you must *accept* yourself.

You must look at all parts of you and you must

accept all parts of you. You are not good, or bad, or ugly, or beautiful. You *are* God.

❧

*A*s long as you are just passing through, you have no desire to hold on to anything in this dimension. As long as you are passing through, you do not need to be attached to what is acted out here. As long as you are passing through you are no longer acting as an owner or a landlord. When you are simply passing through you begin to see how you are simply a caretaker for a very brief moment in time.

If you wish to own this dimension, how can you possibly move on to ascend into fourth and fifth dimensional beingness? If you wish to own, or hook on to, or attach yourself to results within this three dimensional world, you will lose part of you here and not go on to the fourth, more ascended viewpoint.

It is your choice you know? You may stay or you my go. You may become stagnant or you may give birth to glory and wisdom. You have repeated this cycle many, many times and now it is time for many of you to assist in the birth of God consciousness into this level. You will raise this entire dimension simply by raising your own level of awareness. At one point in creation *all* levels of consciousness come together to form the eternal mind of God. This level of consciousness is achievable within the realms of your existence. Everything is achievable within the realms of your existence. Nothing is impossible; nothing is 'not' attainable.

You will find that the more you want and ask for assistance, the more readily you will receive. You will not always see this assistance for its true value, as God's ways are not man's ways, and for some, God does not exist in man. You will find that it is most important to allow all possibilities to exist, for in this you will receive your greatest gifts.

You are not the ones who chose to be here. The fall was simply an experiment, an observation if you will. The fall was not meant to imprison you here. You were meant to reign as the glory in which you were created indicates. You are the light and the glory and the power. You are not some tiny speck who has no significance. You are the birth of God into new life, new awareness, new consciousness. You are but a fragment of your total identity at this moment. You are focused in one area of creation and you are in many areas at this moment.

Shift your focus. Move your attention and you will see how nothing really exists for you. Today you are a banker; tomorrow you are living on the street. Today you focus on deadlines and meetings; tomorrow you focus on the sun warming your body and how you will eat. It is all variables of the same extreme. You are focusing outside of you for your needs and wants. Begin to focus inside of you. Begin to know you and you will lose your fear of loss, because you will find your core, and your core glows like a bright light to welcome you home. You cannot get lost and you cannot lose, for you are always right here inside. You are God. Your center is truth and you know... you really do *know*....

When you begin to lower into a world as dense as this third dimension, you cannot help but be affected by this density. You are here to assist in lightening this situation and you are here to rise above it. You are not meant to suffer and you are not meant to judge. You did not come here to become part of it so much as you came here to visit – to travel through. There are many yet unexplored areas of this and other universes, but I do not expect you to rush in and change them all.

You are here on a mission. Your soul came for a purpose and if you will just get out of the way long enough to allow spirit to take over, you will begin to know why you are here. You did not decide to come just to make a lot of money to leave to others, and you did not decide to come to win at your profession, and you did not decide to come to have a big family. These are situations that are decided upon as you go, but they are not your purpose for being here.

Believe it or not you all have the same purpose. That purpose is to bring forth light. How can you bring forth light if you have not found your light switch? Begin to discover how you work. Begin to open to your own truth. Your center *is* light. You must reach into you to find your center. The trick is that when you reach into the center for your light you will expose your darkness. Your ugliness and your worthlessness and your self-loathing and your anger and hate are all within you, and it is time to move them out.

As you reach into your inner realms you will find much of what you have been hiding from. All your fears and upsets come from this place. It is best to move very gently when you are moving within these realms. It is not always painful, but it is sometimes very confusing for you to face these parts of you. You will find that the majority of you is missing and sits in the darkness. As you turn on your light you will expose these parts of you. You will be forced to deal with your own demons, or evil. You cannot move to the light and not awaken all parts of you. When you begin to see what has slept in you, do not judge yourself for "carrying." Simply allow yourself the time it takes to let-go-of and heal.

All anger must leave. We must see anger for what it is and allow it to transform to its proper perspective. You may change anger into peace by allowing calm to set in. Anger is a state; a projected fear; fear that is so out of control that it is frustrated and comes out with great force. Often it is accompanied by body movement – be it hitting, kicking or other gestures. Anger is at the top of your list to clear. This is due to the fact that anger has been misplaced and denied. You do not trust your anger and so you deny that you are angry.

You may help yourself at this point, by writing down *everything* that upsets you even a little. Then you may begin to ask for the reason each thing upsets you, and how you can change your perspective on seeing it differently. This only works, of course, if you have done your second and third grade lessons and began channeling your soul, or God. If you have accomplished this you may now channel all parts of you, even your anger. Ask why you are upset and allow the words to flow. You will soon see how you do not wish to be in your current state of non-repair.

It is time to heal the world my friend. It begins and it ends right here in you. You may raise the consciousness one thousand fold by simply letting your own self be in the light. You come into the light by admitting you are in darkness and by allowing your darkness to dissolve into light particles. You may heal all of you by simply accepting all of you, and then you will have accomplished your purpose here. You came here to bring light into a very dark area and now you have the opportunity to light up and heal the world by your singular experience.

If you do nothing more than allow yourself to heal, you will have served your purpose on this planet. You are here to transform from darkness to light. You are here to be born into God. You are here to know love. You are here to exist as a light beam that connects to every other light beam. You are not alone in this, but do not be afraid to stand alone.

As you begin to rise up you will know you have completed your purpose. It is often wondered what you are here for and why you came. This is the simplest way to explain it at this time. Later, of course, you will have greater insight and higher understanding. But for now, this is how you will see it: You are simply a light learning how to turn yourself on!

❧

*A*s you begin to grow in God's light you begin to know how you have harmed yourself by your thoughts and your beliefs. Most of your beliefs are old and frozen in place. You are now shifting those old frozen beliefs and learning to accept what you are. You are basically truth and delighted joy and uncompromising wisdom. You are a child of God. You are light being born.

As you begin to see your own good you will begin to know wisdom. You will begin to know grace and you will begin to see how light is born. You will walk above the clouds and you will know that you are indeed God in transition. As you begin to wake to the fact that you are good and innocent you will find a new freedom. As you face your demons (your fears) you will find that they are unfounded and based on illusion. What you see outside is the illusion. What you see within is God's house and God's truth. Ignore the outer reflection and move to the inner realms. Spend your time in peace and joy and let go of any judgment concerning rightness or wrongness. Float within and stay in touch with God. Be alive for yourself and do not live for others. Be your own source.

As you move into your own core you will find that you are no longer afraid. You have seen you for what you are and accepted yourself, and in acceptance of self comes forgiveness and peace of mind. As you move from accepting yourself to loving, you will feel a great release of weight from within. You will finally have reached your own light. As you move into your own light allow yourself the space to know it and love it. You will find that you become enamored with your own self. This is not arrogance; this is *self-love.* Self-love is very powerful and very heady. You will learn to love you as you have never been loved before. You *are* love, and love is what you are.

The end for now….

God's Pen

I first heard the voice of God in 1988. I was sitting in my back yard reading a book when this big booming voice interrupted with, "I am God and I will not come to you by any other name." I felt like the voice was everywhere – inside of me as well as in the sky around me. I was so frightened that I ran in my bedroom to hide.

This was not the first time that I heard voices. I had been communicating with my own spirit guide or soul for about a year. I guess my depth of fear regarding God, and all that he represented to me at the time, was just too much.

I spent two days trying to avoid the voice of God, which was patiently waiting for me to respond. By the second day I was exhausted from lack of sleep and decided to give in and talk with him. This turned out to be the greatest gift and best decision of my life.

The first book, *God Spoke through Me to Tell You to Speak to Him*, shows my evolution from communicating with my soul to communicating with the Big Guy. It took a couple years for me to be comfortable communicating with God. My fear of a punishing God was big! That has most definitely changed and I now think of God as my partner and best friend.

In the beginning the voice of God would wake me in the middle of the night and tell me it was time to write. He said I had promised to do this work (I assumed he was talking about the soul/spirit me). I would drag myself up to a sitting position and watch in amazement as my hand flew across the page, while I tried to keep up by reading what was being written.

It was always so much fun to wake up the next morning and grab my notebook to see what God had written during the night. After some time the voice stopped waking me and I became comfortable picking up my pen and writing for God first thing in the morning. I think in the beginning I had to be awakened while still semi-conscious from sleep so I wouldn't object too much to the information that was being channeled through me.

As I grew less and less afraid (and more trusting) of God, he was able to communicate greater information. Some of the information is quit controversial, but I felt it important to just let it be and not censor it. I present the writings here to you as they were given to me. I have edited a little (mostly the more personal information regarding myself) and I have used a pen name for privacy reasons. I asked God for a good pen name and he guided me to Liane which (I was told) in Hebrew means "God has answered."

At one point I became a little concerned about my sanity in all this, so I went to a hypnotherapist to find out what I was doing. Under hypnosis I saw this incredibly huge beam of light with a voice coming from within it. It was a giant "loving light" and felt so comforting and kind. It felt like that's where I came from. After that I stopped worrying about my sanity. If this is crazy, I think it's a very good kind of crazy to be....

In loving light, Liane

Loving Light Books

Available at:
Loving Light Books: www.lovinglightbooks.com
Amazon: www.amazon.com
Barnes & Noble: www.barnesandnoble.com

Also Available on Request at Local Bookstores

www.ingramcontent.com/pod-product-compliance
Lightning Source LLC
LaVergne TN
LVHW090947080826
845145LV00003B/925

* 9 7 8 1 8 7 8 4 8 0 1 0 1 *